BBC
DOCTOR WHO DW

THE OFFICIAL
QUIZ
BOOK

BBC
DOCTOR WHO
THE OFFICIAL
QUIZ
BOOK

Jacqueline Rayner

BBC
BOOKS

1 3 5 7 9 10 8 6 4 2

Published in 2014 by BBC Books, an imprint of Ebury Publishing
A Random House Group Company

The Random House Group Limited Reg. No. 954009

Addresses for companies within the Random House Group
can be found at www.randomhouse.co.uk

A CIP catalogue record for this book is available from the British Library.

ISBN 978 1 849 90769 9

Editorial director: Albert DePetrillo
Series consultant: Justin Richards
Project editor: Steve Tribe
Cover design: Lee Binding © Woodlands Books Ltd, 2014
Production: Alex Goddard

Printed and bound in the USA

To buy books by your favourite authors and register for offers,
visit www.randomhouse.co.uk

Contents

Dedicated to Andrew Pixley,
knowledgeable and generous King of Facts

Notes on Terminology

The quizzes in this book cover the stories from *An Unearthly Child* (1963) to *The Time of the Doctor* (2013) and feature both the fiction of *Doctor Who* and the series' behind-the-scenes events and personnel.

There is at least one question relating to every single televised story. Questions may, very occasionally, reference an untransmitted / unmade story / episode, but books, audios, comics, animation, films and other non-televisual media are not included.

If one of the quiz questions was 'name all the Doctor's companions', it's likely that no two people would come up with the same answer! So to avoid confusion (although it may cause some disagreement), herein we're counting the following companions, assistants, close colleagues, wives, associates and one-off wonders as 'companions': Susan, Ian, Barbara, Vicki, Steven, Katarina, Sara, Dodo, Polly, Ben, Jamie, Victoria, Zoe, Liz, the Brigadier, Benton, Yates, Jo, Sarah Jane, Harry, Leela, K-9 Mk 1, K-9 Mk 2, Romana 1, Romana 2, Adric, Nyssa, Tegan, Turlough, Kamelion, Peri, Mel, Ace, Grace, Chang Lee, Rose, Adam, Mickey, Captain Jack, Donna, Martha, Astrid, River Song, Jackson Lake, Lady Christina, Adelaide, Wilf, Amy, Rory and Clara.

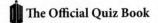

Several stories have disputed titles. In this book we are using:

Serial A: *An Unearthly Child*

Serial B: *The Daleks*

Serial C: *The Edge of Destruction*

Serial T/A: *Mission to the Unknown*

Serial W: *The Massacre*

Serial 7A: *The Mysterious Planet*

Serial 7B: *Mindwarp*

Serial 7C (first four episodes): *Terror of the Vervoids*

Serial 7C (last two episodes): *The Ultimate Foe*

Again, this is to avoid confusion, rather than being a pronouncement on correct nomenclature.

THE QUESTIONS

Each quiz of fifteen questions is divided into three sections of escalating difficulty:

Questions 1–5: Jericho Street Junior
A new viewer or more casual fan? These questions are the ones for you.

Questions 6–10: Coal Hill School
Fancy something a bit more challenging? Have a go at these questions.

Questions 11–15: Time Lord Academy
So, you think you really know your stuff? Test yourself with the trickiest questions.

As the Fourth Doctor once said: 'Good luck, my dears!'

Pre-Titles Sequence

A few questions on Doctor Who *basics to get you in
the mood for what's to follow…*

The Doctors

Who played:

1. The Tenth Doctor?
2. The Fourth Doctor?
3. The Third Doctor?
4. The Eleventh Doctor?
5. The Twelfth Doctor?

6. The Fifth Doctor?
7. The Second Doctor?
8. The Sixth Doctor?
9. The First Doctor?
10. The Seventh Doctor?

11. The Ninth Doctor?
12. The Eighth Doctor?
13. The War Doctor?
14. The Valeyard?
15. The First Doctor in *The Five Doctors*?

The Companions 1

Who played:

1. Donna Noble?
2. Amy Pond?
3. Brigadier Alistair Lethbridge-Stewart?
4. Jamie Macrimmon?
5. Mickey Smith?

6. Ian Chesterton?
7. Vicki?
8. Jo Grant?
9. Peri Brown?
10. Zoe Heriot?

11. Sara Kingdom?
12. Nyssa?
13. Ben Jackson?
14. Grace Holloway?
15. Sergeant Benton?

The Companions 2

Who played:

1. Rose Tyler?
2. River Song?
3. Clara Oswald?
4. Wilf Mott?
5. Sarah Jane Smith?

6. Susan Foreman?
7. Victoria Waterfield?
8. Romana 1?
9. Melanie Bush?
10. Liz Shaw?

11. Steven Taylor?
12. Harry Sullivan?
13. Katarina?
14. Adric?
15. Turlough?

The Companions 3

Who played:

1. Leela?
2. Martha Jones?
3. Captain Jack Harkness?
4. Rory Williams?
5. Ace?

6. K-9 (original voice)?
7. Romana 2?
8. Tegan Jovanka?
9. Barbara Wright?
10. Polly?

11. Dodo Chaplet?
12. Kamelion (voice)?
13. Captain Mike Yates?
14. Adam Mitchell?
15. Chang Lee?

Talkin' 'bout Regeneration

1. In which story does the First Doctor regenerate?
2. In which story does the Second Doctor regenerate?
3. In which story does the Third Doctor regenerate?
4. In which story does the Fourth Doctor regenerate?
5. In which story does the Fifth Doctor regenerate?

6. In which story does the Sixth Doctor regenerate?
7. In which story does the Ninth Doctor regenerate?
8. In which story does the Tenth Doctor regenerate?
9. In which story does the Eleventh Doctor regenerate?
10. In which story does the Seventh Doctor regenerate?

11. In which story does the War Doctor regenerate?
12. In which mini-episode does the Eighth Doctor regenerate?
13. Which is the first story in which the word 'regenerate' is used to describe the Time Lords' process of change?
14. Which two companions of the Doctor have also regenerated?
15. From where in the Doctor's timeline does the Valeyard come?

Hello, Goodbye 1

Which companion or companions' (main) tenure spanned:

1. *An Unearthly Child* to *The Dalek Invasion of Earth?*
2. *Smith and Jones* to *The Last of the Time Lords?*
3. *The Keeper of Traken* to *Terminus?*
4. *Terror of the Autons* to *The Green Death?*
5. *The Highlanders* to *The War Games?*

6. *Planet of Fire* to *Mindwarp?*
7. *Robot* to *Terror of the Zygons?*
8. *Mawdryn Undead* to *Planet of Fire?*
9. *The Ribos Operation* to *The Armageddon Factor?*
10. *Logopolis* to *Resurrection of the Daleks?*

11. *The War Machines* to *The Faceless Ones?*
12. *The Invisible Enemy* to *The Invasion of Time?*
13. *The Chase* to *The Savages?*
14. *The Myth Makers* to *The Daleks' Master Plan?*
15. *The King's Demons* to *Planet of Fire?*

Hello, Goodbye 2

Which companion or companions' (main) tenure spanned:

1. *Rose* to *Doomsday?*
2. *Full Circle* to *Earthshock?*
3. *Partners in Crime* to *Journey's End?*
4. *Dragonfire* to *Survival?*
5. *An Unearthly Child* to *The Chase?*

6. *The Time Warrior* to *The Hand of Fear?*
7. *Spearhead from Space* to *Inferno?*
8. *The Face of Evil* to *The Invasion of Time?*
9. *Destiny of the Daleks* to *Warriors' Gate?*
10. *The Rescue* to *The Myth Makers?*

11. *Terror of the Vervoids* to *Dragonfire?*
12. *Dalek* to *The Long Game?*
13. *The Daleks' Master Plan* only?
14. *The Massacre* to *The War Machines?*
15. *The Wheel in Space* to *The War Games?*

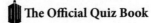

Personal Possessions 1

Which Doctor is most associated with:

1. A very long scarf?
2. A stick of celery?
3. A question-mark jumper?
4. A cat badge?
5. A fez?

6. A leather jacket?
7. Jelly babies?
8. A bow tie?
9. A velvet smoking jacket?
10. A question-mark umbrella?

11. A 500-year diary?
12. A blue-stone ring?
13. Half-moon glasses?
14. Perfectly fitting shoes?
15. A trench coat?

Personal Possessions 2

Which companion is most associated with:

1. A badge for mathematical excellence?
2. A leaf?
3. A kilt?
4. Nitro-9?
5. A police uniform?

6. Janis thorns?
7. Roman armour?
8. A vortex manipulator?
9. A silver catsuit?
10. Memory wafers?

11. A swagger stick?
12. A ballgown?
13. A tiara?
14. A toy owl?
15. A toy panda?

Name That Story 1

Identify the following stories from their initials:

1. BO
2. H
3. POG
4. MP
5. CT

6. POTS
7. SOD
8. AOTD
9. TROT
10. TUD

11. TCH
12. THON
13. TATM
14. THE
15. TAC

Name That Story 2

Identify the following stories from their initials:

1. COM
2. CB
3. HN
4. DOTM
5. WG

6. COD
7. NIS
8. DOAS
9. TIP
10. DIM

11. TUM
12. TEOT
13. TUATW
14. TOTA
15. TPOT

Title Hunt 1

Identify the (1963–1989) *Doctor Who* story from the number of letters in each word of its title:

1. 9
2. 7
3. 6
4. 3, 3
5. 5, 5

6. 7, 6
7. 7, 2, 3, 7
8. 4, 4, 3, 4
9. 6, 2, 3, 7
10. 3, 8, 4, 2, 3, 6

11. 3, 3, 7
12. 3, 9, 5
13. 3, 5, 9
14. 3, 4, 2, 3, 6
15. 3, 7, 2, 7

Title Hunt 2

Identify the (2005–2013) *Doctor Who* story from the number of letters in each word of its title:

1. 6
2. 3, 5
3. 5, 7
4. 7, 4
5. 1, 9, 5

6. 7, 2, 3, 6, 2, 3, 6
7. 9, 2, 3, 6
8. 3, 7, 8
9. 8, 2, 5
10. 3, 4, 6

11. 3, 9, 5
12. 6, 2, 6
13. 4, 2, 6
14. 3, 6, 3
15. 7, 2, 3, 7

Births and Birthdays

1. What is the Second Doctor's first full story?
2. What is the Third Doctor's first story?
3. What is the Fourth Doctor's first full story?
4. What is the Fifth Doctor's first full story?
5. What is the Sixth Doctor's first full story?

6. What is the Seventh Doctor's first story?
7. What is the Ninth Doctor's first story?
8. What is the Tenth Doctor's first full story?
9. What is the Eleventh Doctor's first full story?
10. What story was made to celebrate ten years of *Doctor Who*?

11. What story was made to celebrate the show's twentieth anniversary?
12. What story was made to celebrate the show's twenty-fifth anniversary?
13. What Children in Need special was made to celebrate the show's thirtieth anniversary?
14. What story was made to celebrate the show's fiftieth anniversary?
15. What was *Doctor Who*'s 100th story?

Opening Titles

Initially – A

1. What A are creatures made from living fat?
2. What A is the planet Adric comes from?
3. What A is the constellation the Sleepers are from?
4. What A is the ruler of Chloris?
5. What A is the sacred beast of Peladon?

6. What A is the horse that goes from eighteenth-century France to a spaceship and back?
7. What A are the eye-like aliens who want Prisoner Zero returned to them?
8. What A is the king whose cup is stolen by Lady Christina de Souza?
9. What A is used to poison the Sensorites' aqueduct?
10. What A is the male Kinda who has voice?

*

11. What A is the goddess worshipped by the people of Atlantis?
12. What A is the name the Tenth Doctor gives to a galaxy before he goes to meet Ood Sigma?
13. What A is the planet the *Empress* is approaching when it crashes into the *Hecate*?
14. What A is a rare mineral used to make space beacons?
15. What A is a friend of Jackie's who got £2,000 compensation because a man at the council said she looked Greek?

Initially – B

1. What B is a living stone imp?
2. What B wants to be President Eternal and rule for ever?
3. What B is a sprightly yellow roadster?
4. What B can be Lance or Koquillion?
5. What B owns the DVD shop where Larry Nightingale works?

6. What B is a ring the Doctor puts on Donna's finger?
7. What B is Captain Wrack's ship?
8. What B believes that what is good for Global Chemicals is good for the world?
9. What B are desperate for grain?
10. What B battles Sir Lancelot in the Land of Fiction?

11. What B is the village where Vivien Fay lives?
12. What B is a ship with a Weeping Angel onboard?
13. What B is the first member of LINDA to be absorbed?
14. What B is the password for the UNIT computer system?
15. What B is Orcini's squire?

Initially – C

1. What C takes in the Doctor as a lodger?
2. What C is the bell that rings when the TARDIS is in danger?
3. What C are cold-loving natives of Telos?
4. What C is a ship controlled by Miss Hartigan?
5. What C is a clone grown by Cassandra?

6. What C is a deadly schoolboy who played games in the Celestial Toyroom?
7. What C does Cessair of Diplos pretend to be?
8. What C is the battle in which Jamie has been fighting just before he meets the Doctor?
9. What C is Captain Pike's first mate?
10. What C is the doctor who cares for the gas-mask zombies?

*

11. What C is a Time Lord who had a snake tattoo in every incarnation?
12. What C is the nickname of the Highland Games champion duplicated by the Zygons?
13. What C kidnaps Martha to get access to the fast lane of the motorway?
14. What C is the colonel who is the Brigadier's replacement at UNIT?
15. What C is the name adopted by the Doctor in *The Gunfighters*?

Episode One
The Doctor and Co

The First Doctor

1. What do Ian and Barbara assume is the Doctor's name when they first meet him?
2. What resemblance does the Doctor claim to see in Dodo when he first meets her?
3. What does Susan say is the Doctor's favourite period of Earth history?
4. Who create a robot double of the Doctor, to 'infiltrate and kill'?
5. Who does Steven mistake for the Doctor in sixteenth-century France?

6. From how many years 'earlier' than the Monk does the Doctor claim to be?
7. To whom does the Doctor lose the TARDIS in a game of backgammon?
8. What mental image does the Doctor project on Lobos's screen after he claims the Doctor is not an amphibian?
9. What does the Doctor tell Doc Holliday he 'never touches'?
10. The Doctor had previously met the 'friendly inhabitants' of which planet?

*

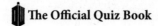

11. On what planet did the Doctor and Susan encounter plants that used thought transference?
12. Who reportedly told the Doctor that he looked better in a cloak?
13. What is the Elders' name for the Doctor?
14. According to Susan, what is in the Doctor's notebook?
15. In which story do we see the First Doctor's library card?

The Second Doctor

1. What doesn't fit the newly regenerated Doctor, leading Ben to believe he's not the Doctor at all?
2. What alias does the Doctor adopt in eighteenth-century Scotland?
3. What do the Krotons call the Doctor?
4. Who accompanies the Second Doctor in the Death Zone on Gallifrey?
5. Who first gives the Doctor the alias 'John Smith'?

6. Who does the Doctor pretend to be on Vulcan?
7. What does the Doctor say is one of the most terrible times on the planet Earth?
8. What does the Doctor use to save Vana from the Kroton's deadly gas?
9. What planet had the Doctor previously visited that was so peaceful he hadn't wanted to leave?
10. What charge do the Time Lords lay against the Doctor?

*

11. What does the Doctor use to booby-trap the floor of Dom Issigri's study?
12. After the Third Doctor has been transported to Omega's world, how does the Brigadier explain the Second Doctor to the Security Council?
13. Why do Anton, Rod and Curly try to kill the Doctor?
14. How does the Doctor restore his usual scruffy appearance in the Colony?
15. On what condition does the Doctor agree to let Jamie travel with him?

The Third Doctor

1. What form of aikido and karate does the Doctor commonly use?
2. Where is the prison to which the Doctor sent when he is believed to be an agent of the Draconians?
3. What does the Keller Machine initially reveal to be the Doctor's greatest fear?
4. Where is the Doctor keeping his TARDIS key when he first arrives on Earth?
5. Who taught the Doctor the techniques he used to escape the Spiders' web-cocoon?

6. How does the Doctor describe himself after he breaks free of a time loop and discovers the TARDIS is programmed always to return to Earth?
7. What two disguises does the Doctor adopt to get inside Global Chemicals?
8. How long does the Doctor tell Liz his life has covered?
9. Who describes the Doctor as 'a long-shanked rascal with a mighty nose'?
10. What game do the Doctor and Jo play while locked up in Stangmoor Prison?

11. In how many stories does the Third Doctor face the Master?
12. What does the Doctor tell Captain Hart he never carries?
13. What does the Doctor make out of, among other things, a wine bottle, forks and tea leaves?
14. What 'spider' does the Doctor surrender to, according to K'Anpo?
15. Whose hat, cloak and car does the Doctor steal from Ashbridge hospital?

The Fourth Doctor

1. What do the Doctor and Sarah use to trip up Eldrad and send him plummeting into the abyss?
2. By what name does Drax know the Doctor?
3. What Time Lord chapter is the Doctor a member of?
4. Why does the Doctor declare himself a presidential candidate while on trial for murder of the President of the Time Lords?
5. Who is the finest swordsman the Doctor ever saw (who showed him a few points)?

6. What sign does the Doctor claim he was born under (really the symbol of the maternity service on Gallifrey)?
7. Where is the bridge through the barrier of the carved Doctor-Xoanon's head?
8. What percentage did the Doctor gain on his second attempt at graduating from the Academy?
9. What is the most important thing the Doctor's cybernetics tutor ever taught him?
10. Who is the first person to whom the Fourth Doctor offers a jelly baby?

*

11. Which society, of which the Doctor is president, finds Krynoids difficult to study?
12. Who once offered a whole star system for the Doctor's head?
13. How old does the Doctor tell Maren he is?
14. How old does Romana believe the Doctor is when she first meets him?
15. How long has the Doctor been operating the TARDIS, according to Romana?

The Fifth Doctor

1. Who uses the Doctor's biodata extract to take on his form?
2. Apart from a gun, what does the Doctor use to destroy the Cyber Leader?
3. What instrument does the Doctor play to open the secret entrance to Borusa's lair?
4. What is the Doctor's last word before he regenerates?
5. What 'old friend' of the Doctor is 'killed' by the Terileptil leader?

6. What costume does the Doctor wear to the Cranleighs' fancy dress ball?
7. How does the Sixth Doctor describe his predecessor to Peri?
8. Why does the Doctor wear a stick of celery?
9. Why would the Doctor not 'be a Time Lord any more' after helping Mawdryn and the mutants?
10. What does Nyssa build out of TARDIS doors to protect the newly regenerated Doctor?

*

11. Why do the Daleks plan to send duplicates of the Doctor, Tegan and Turlough to Gallifrey?
12. Why does the Doctor refuse the prize of enlightenment?
13. What place does Tegan tell the Terileptil leader she thinks the Doctor may be from?
14. What does the Garm ask the Doctor to do for him?
15. Who at UNIT does the Doctor refer Heathrow's Security officers to?

The Sixth Doctor

1. Which old friend and mentor does the Doctor meet on Jaconda?
2. Who had been a captain when the Doctor met him previously?
3. What long-overdue repair work does the Doctor undertake shortly before arriving on Earth, 1985?
4. What dietary lifestyle does the Doctor say he is going to adopt after his meeting with the Androgums?
5. What new charge does the Valeyard call to be laid against the Doctor following the destruction of the Vervoids?

6. Why is the Doctor no longer President of Gallifrey?
7. What colour cravat does the Doctor wear during his encounter with the Vervoids?
8. When it is suggested that the Doctor stands for Lord President again, who does he suggest should stand instead?
9. What method of death awaits the Doctor after he is accused of water theft on Ravolox?
10. Whose funeral does the Doctor intend to attend on Necros?

*

11. On what asteroid does the Doctor plan to become a hermit?
12. Where is the Doctor on his way to when the TARDIS is drawn off course to Killingworth?
13. Who calls the Doctor a 'foul fanged fiend'?
14. Whose dying words sent the Doctor to Thoros Beta?
15. What is the title of the thesis the Doctor said he might stay on Ravalox for a year to write?

The Seventh Doctor

1. What does the Doctor hate, as well as bus stations, unrequited love, tyranny and cruelty?
2. What is the Doctor's favourite kind of jazz?
3. What do time and tide do, according to the Doctor?
4. What figure from Arthurian myth is the Doctor revealed to be?
5. What old possession does the Brigadier have taken out of mothballs for the Doctor?

6. Who claims to be the only person to know who the Doctor really is?
7. What does the Doctor mutter to create a barrier of faith against the Haemovores?
8. During his show for the Gods of Ragnarok, what does the Doctor turn a snake into?
9. What injury leads to the Doctor's regeneration?
10. What is the Doctor's prize for being the tollbooth's ten-billionth customer?

*

11. How old are both the Doctor and the Rani at the time they met on Lakertya?
12. What colour scarf do the Kangs give the Doctor?
13. What is in the centre of the Doctor's calling card?
14. How many years' experience does the Doctor claim to have in rewiring alien machinery?
15. What sort of honey does Goronwy give the Doctor as a farewell present?

The Eighth Doctor

1. What alias does Grace give the Doctor?
2. What does the Doctor say will be destroyed if he looks into the Eye of Harmony?
3. What fancy dress costume does the Doctor take from the hospital?
4. What 'almost destroys' the Doctor's regenerative process?
5. Whose shoes does Grace give the Doctor?

6. What do the Doctor and Grace use to get down from the top of the Institute for Technological Advancement and Research building?
7. Where does the Doctor always leave a spare TARDIS key?
8. What film is showing on the TV in the hospital morgue when the Doctor regenerates?
9. How much weight does the Doctor lose in 20 minutes?
10. Who does the Doctor claim to have known intimately?

*

11. Where is Grace when she is called to operate on the wounded Doctor?
12. Which question does the Doctor tell Gareth to answer in his mid-term exam?
13. What does the Doctor steal from the Institute for Technological Advancement and Research?
14. How far is Gallifrey from Earth, according to the Doctor?
15. And how long would it take the TARDIS to travel that far?

The Ninth Doctor

1. Whose website reads 'DOCTOR WHO? Have you seen this man?'?
2. What does the Doctor use to attack Auton Mickey in a restaurant?
3. What gift does the Doctor offer the guests on Platform One?
4. What name does the Doctor insist on calling Mickey?
5. Nine hundred years of time travel, and what had never happened to the Doctor before he met Rose?

6. On Satellite Five, who calls the Doctor her lucky charm?
7. Who does the psychic paper say the Doctor is when the TARDIS lands in 1941?
8. What does the Doctor say setting 2,428 on the sonic screwdriver does?
9. In what newspaper does the Doctor spot Margaret-Slitheen's photo?
10. What does Captain Jack think is the Doctor's name when he first meets him?

*

11. What is the Doctor called in the ancient legends of the Dalek homeworld?
12. How many languages does the Doctor tell the Daleks he can speak?
13. What does the Emperor Dalek call the Doctor?
14. Where and when have the Doctor, Rose and Captain Jack been shortly before finding themselves on the Game Station?
15. What injury of the Doctor's is healed by the nanogenes in WWII London?

The Tenth Doctor

1.   What part of the Doctor is cut off by the Sycorax leader?
2.   What are the Tenth Doctor's last words?
3.   What item of clothing does the Doctor remove, the first time Martha sees him?
4.   What does the Doctor use to turn himself human?
5.   What process creates the DoctorDonna?

6.   Who tells the Doctor that his song must end soon?
7.   What 'heals the synapses' of the newly regenerated Doctor?
8.   What title does Queen Victoria bestow on the Doctor?
9.   What subject does the Doctor teach at Deffry Vale School?
10. What drink does the Doctor claim to have invented 'a few centuries early'?

*

11. Whose mother did the Doctor fail to save from an elemental shade?
12. According to the Doctor, what day does he never land on?
13. What does the Doctor tell Jackson Lake that all his companions do in the end?
14. Who does the security guard at the Alexandra Palace studios think the Doctor is?
15. What does the Doctor call himself after saving Adelaide Brooke?

The Eleventh Doctor

1. What is the Doctor called by the Arwells?
2. What does the Doctor call the TARDIS when they're alone?
3. What is Ada Gillyflower's name for the Doctor?
4. What does the Doctor pretend is a TARDIS self-destruct button?
5. What monster body part is the Doctor's friend 'Handles'?

6. What is the Doctor's Rule One?
7. What is the Doctor's other Rule One?
8. Who are the members of the Doctor's gang that Amy worries are 'the new us'?
9. Who does the Doctor pretend to be when visiting Dr Simeon?
10. What does the Doctor think is the only mystery worth solving?

*

11. What does the Doctor see inside 'his' room in The God Complex?
12. What food does the Doctor crave immediately after regenerating?
13. What does alternative-timeline Winston Churchill call the Doctor?
14. What does the Doctor owe Casanova following a bet?
15. How does the Doctor pass information from his mind to Craig's?

Don't Give up the Day Job

At the time they begin their travels with the Doctor, which of his companions is:

1. A kissogram?
2. A medical student?
3. An air hostess?
4. A journalist?
5. A piper?

6. A sailor?
7. An SSS agent?
8. A history teacher?
9. A science teacher?
10. UNIT's Medical Officer?

11. A botany student?
12. A computer programmer?
13. A nurse?
14. A space pilot?
15. A librarian?

What's in a Name?

1. What is Ace's real first name?
2. What is Dodo's real first name?
3. What surname does Susan adopt during her time at Coal Hill School?
4. What is Turlough's first name?
5. Which companion's name is an anagram of 'TARDIS'?

6. What is Peri's real first name?
7. Which companion becomes Mrs Jones after her marriage?
8. What was Captain Jack's nickname when he was young?
9. What is Jamie's middle name?
10. What is River Song's name at birth?

11. What is Amy's middle name?
12. Sergeant Benton's first name is never given on screen, but what is it generally accepted to be?
13. What is Rory's middle name?
14. What is Jackie Tyler's maiden name?
15. Rose's middle name is never given on screen, but what is it according to creator Russell T Davies?

Relative Dimensions

Which companion has:

1. A 'high-up' uncle?
2. A grandfather who is also a companion of the Doctor?
3. An aunt who is a renowned virologist?
4. A brother whom she kills?
5. A time-travelling antiques-dealer father?

6. A baby brother called Tony?
7. An archaeologist stepfather?
8. A father who takes the Test of the Horda in her place?
9. A father who lost everything when the Icelandic banks collapsed?
10. A grandmother who was a radio operator in the Second World War?

11. A descendant who fell in love with a Trandorian prince and created a new species?
12. A father who was murdered after a spaceship crash?
13. A great aunt who 'wouldn't care if she never saw her again'?
14. A grandfather who lives in Little Hodcombe?
15. A dad who went off to Spain and never came back?

Companions – The First Doctor

1. Who does Barbara pretend to be after the TARDIS lands in an Aztec tomb?
2. Who is Katarina handmaiden to?
3. Who does Steven think Dodo may be descended from?
4. Who cuts Steven's hair for him?
5. What zoo did Dodo once visit with her school?

6. What planet was Vicki travelling to when her ship crashed on Dido?
7. What colour is Ian's Coal Hill School tie?
8. Who gave Barbara the bracelet that enables the Zarbi to control her?
9. How long is Steven trapped on Mechanus?
10. How long has Susan been in twentieth-century England at the time of *An Unearthly Child*?

*

11. UNIT's Black Archive contains a photo of Sara Kingdom with which other person?
12. What two locations does Steven see himself in on the Toymaker's hypnotic screen?
13. For whose murder is Ian sentenced to death in Millennius?
14. With whom does Barbara have a brief romance in revolutionary France?
15. According to the writing on Ben's cap, what ship does he serve on?

Companions – The Second Doctor

1. What is Ben's nickname for Polly?
2. Which Doctor adopts the alias 'Dr James Macrimmon'?
3. Why, according to the Daleks, was Jamie chosen for the Human Factor tests?
4. Illusions of which of his companions does the Second Doctor encounter in the Death Zone?
5. The Doctor shows Zoe thought patterns featuring which monster, to make sure she wants to join the TARDIS crew?

6. What was the name of Jamie's father?
7. Just before the TARDIS lands near an extinct volcano, where and when does Polly hope they will land?
8. What name is used by Polly's Chameleon double?
9. What 'lovely pudding' does Victoria tell Griffin she used to have at home?
10. When Jamie first sees a Cyberman, what does he think it is?

*

11. Where does Zoe work on the Wheel?
12. What gift does Tobias Vaughn give Jamie?
13. What did Ben live opposite when he was 'a kid'?
14. Which two companions pretend to be boyfriend and girlfriend to infiltrate an enemy base?
15. What are the ingredients of Cocktail Polly?

Companions – The Third Doctor

1. Who is Sarah Jane pretending to be when she first meets the Doctor?
2. What does the Doctor use to clear Mike's mind from BOSS's mind-conditioning?
3. What rank does Elizabeth Shaw hold in the parallel Earth?
4. What title does the Doctor bestow on Jo when introducing her to King Peladon?
5. Who asks Jo to go back to Skaro with him?

6. Who asks Benton to join her in a fertility dance?
7. Which two Third Doctor companions do we never see enter the TARDIS?
8. What role does Mike Yates assume to infiltrate Global Chemicals?
9. Who does a later Doctor give Liz's UNIT pass to?
10. What is the first alien world Jo visits?

*

11. What is the second favour Jo asks her uncle for?
12. What magazine does Sarah Jane work for?
13. What present did Doris give the Brigadier in Brighton to 'mark her gratitude'?
14. What is the Brigadier's call sign at the time of the first World Peace Conference?
15. How old is Sarah Jane at the time of her arrest in deserted London?

Companions – The Fourth Doctor

1. In what universe does the Doctor meet Adric?
2. What drink does Sarah hate?
3. What year does Sarah tell Laurence Scarman she's from?
4. What are Leela's toxic weapons of choice?
5. What causes Leela's eye colour to change?

6. What does Harry plan to do with gold from Voga?
7. What subject does K-9 erase from his memory banks after taking Romana literally?
8. In what Gallifreyan bureau did Romana work for a time?
9. What illness is K-9 suffering from while the Doctor and Romana are encountering Daleks?
10. What does Keara give Adric after his brother Varsh's death?

*

11. How many levels of intensity does K-9's photon-beam weaponry have?
12. After the Zygon defeat, what form of transport does Harry opt for instead of going to London in the TARDIS?
13. What aspect of Princess Astra's body is the regenerating Romana not satisfied with?
14. How old does Romana tell Duggan she is?
15. Where does the Doctor tell Professor Litefoot that Leela was found?

Companions – The Fifth Doctor

1. What did Tegan eat when she was 3, but didn't like the taste?
2. How does Tegan describe herself to Lieutenant Scott?
3. Who did Tegan go to Amsterdam to meet?
4. Of whom is Nyssa the exact double?
5. Who recruits Turlough to kill the Doctor?

6. Before being found by the Master, Kamelion was the tool of an invader of which planet?
7. What mark does Turlough have on his arm?
8. How do Nyssa and Tegan realise the Adric they encounter on prehistoric Earth is an illusion?
9. What does Turlough use to threaten the orderlies on Frontios to stop them killing the Doctor?
10. Why did the Doctor get the Tegan 'android' cheap, according to what he told the Gravis?

*

11. What does the Doctor 'rig up' for Nyssa after she faints?
12. The newly regenerated Doctor appoints Tegan as the co-ordinator, but what role does he assign to Adric?
13. What is Tegan's flight number?
14. What country is Peri planning to travel to before she meets the Doctor?
15. What is Turlough's Trion rank?

Companions – The Sixth Doctor

1. What sort of creature does Peri turn into after undergoing the cell mutation experiment on Varos?
2. Who – or what – prevents Peri stepping on one of the Rani's mines?
3. What drink does Mel make the Doctor drink?
4. What does Peri tell Yrcanos are her name and title?
5. What village did Mel live in before travelling with the Doctor?

6. What excuse does Peri give for calling at Dona Arana's hacienda?
7. What fate does the Borad plan for Peri?
8. What almost makes Peri feel homesick on Necros?
9. According to the Doctor, Mel has a memory like what creature?
10. Who attacks Peri on Space Station Camera?

*

11. Which names of past companions does the not-long-regenerated Doctor call Peri?

12. What plant does Peri pick on Necros, with which to 'wow her college' on her return to Earth?

13. What fate nearly claims Mel after she's rendered unconscious on the *Hyperion III*?

14. What is Peri looking for in Redfern Dell?

15. What attacks Peri in a cliffside cave on Thoros Beta?

Companions – The Seventh Doctor

1. What is Ace's job when she first meets the Doctor?
2. Who becomes Ace's 'sister'?
3. What is Ace's nickname for Mel?
4. What is Ace's nickname for the Doctor?
5. What does Ace use to attack the Daleks?

6. What do Tabby and Tilda use to attack Mel?
7. What does Mel claim is her middle name, while talking to Delta?
8. How old was Ace when she burned down Gabriel Chase?
9. What writer's works does Mel admire?
10. What does Sorin give Ace, to replace her fake one?

11. Aces are rare – in comparison, what are easy to come by, according to the Seventh Doctor?
12. What football team does Ace support?
13. What item of clothing belonging to the Doctor does Ace try on while searching for her rucksack?
14. Which teacher at Ace's school mistook home-made gelignite for plasticine?
15. Where in London does Ace's nan live?

Companions – The Eighth Doctor

1. What is Grace's nickname at the hospital?
2. What opera is Grace watching when she's summoned to the hospital?
3. According to the Doctor, Grace is 'tired of life, but' – what?
4. How does the Master refer to Chang Lee?
5. What is Grace's medical area of expertise?

6. What colour do Grace's eyes turn when she is possessed?
7. What does the Master open with Chang Lee's help?
8. How does the Master kill Chang Lee?
9. What name does Chang Lee give to the Doctor for the ambulance paperwork?
10. What does Chang Lee try to give back to the Doctor but is told to keep?

11. What is Chang Lee's first answer when the Master asks him what he'd want if he could have anything in the world?
12. What does Grace shoot with the cop's gun?
13. What part of Grace's body gets hit with the Master's slime?
14. When must Chang Lee take a vacation, according to the Doctor?
15. What hospital does Grace work at?

Companions – The Ninth Doctor

1. What does Rose ask Mickey to bring to Cardiff for her?
2. What show does Rose find herself taking part in on the Game Station?
3. After leaving Platform One, what does Rose decide she wants?
4. What does Mickey use to try to open the TARDIS console?
5. What design features on the T-shirt Rose wears in 1941?

6. Where does Jackie suggest Rose could get a job after her shop blew up?
7. The Doctor came first in jiggery-pokery; what did Rose fail?
8. What does Adam have installed at the same time as his info-spike?
9. What does Captain Jack think Rose is when he first meets her?
10. There's a price on Captain Jack's head in how many solar systems?

*

11. What is 'our song' for Rose and Captain Jack?
12. What two items does Jack combine to make himself a gun on the Game Station?
13. How did Adam nearly cause World War Three when he was 8?
14. What does Rose tell Pete he does every Saturday in the future?
15. When Rose returns home thinking she's only been gone twelve hours, who does she say she'd been staying with overnight?

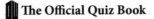

Companions – The Tenth Doctor

1. Who does Martha marry?
2. What hospital is Martha a student at when she first meets the Doctor?
3. What job does Rose have at Deffry Vale High School?
4. In which district of London was Donna born?
5. What two words does Rose tell Donna to say to the Doctor?

6. On whose ship does Wilf man an asteroid laser?
7. What far-off land does the Doctor tell Shakespeare that Martha's from?
8. Who calls Donna 'the nice lady'?
9. What does Dalek Caan call the Doctor's companions?
10. What does Lady Christina use to pay her bus fare?

11. In which story is Martha given her own TARDIS key?
12. Who says of the TARDIS 'the blue box is kind of small, but… I could squeeze in. Like a stowaway'?
13. Who does Donna marry in the world of the Library?
14. What is the name of Jackson Lake's son?
15. On what date does Adelaide Brooke die?

Companions – The Eleventh Doctor

1. How long passes for Amelia while she waits for the Doctor to return after 'five minutes'?
2. What hairstyle does Rory adopt in the Dream Lord's Leadworth?
3. How does River save the Doctor's life after her attempted murder of him?
4. Who does Idris think of as 'the pretty one'?
5. What is Auton Rory known as while he guards the Pandorica?

6. What perfume does Amy advertise?
7. While in the Dalek asylum, what does Amy reveal as the reason she split up with Rory?
8. What are the names of the two children Clara looks after?
9. What was Clara's mother's name?
10. Who proposes marriage to Clara?

*

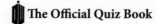

11. What are the last words Clara says to the Doctor before he regenerates?
12. What shop does Amy's enemy stand outside with a Jack Russell?
13. What is Rory's favourite type of car?
14. What does the vision of Amy say to the Doctor before he regenerates?
15. What date is Rory originally sent back to by the New York Weeping Angels?

Could've Been, Should've Been

1. Which Liverpudlian would have become a 1960s companion if the actress hadn't turned down the offer?
2. Which companion thinks he is the Doctor?
3. Which Season 24 character was one of two prospective companions, but lost out to Ace?
4. Who is told by the Doctor to 'give me two minutes. Pack a bag' as he plans to take her to see the stars?
5. Which surrogate companion has the philosophy 'if it moves, hit it'?

6. Which surrogate companion is (presumably) inspired to write science fiction by his adventures with the Doctor?
7. Which monster travels in the TARDIS to Kolkokron (and who knows, maybe has many adventures along the way)?
8. Which surrogate companion sees one companion die before being killed by another?
9. Which character was to have been a companion, but was instead replaced by her supposed descendant?
10. Who gets a lift in the TARDIS to 1643 after an adventure with the Doctor?

*

11. Which surrogate companion is told 'maybe she could' go with the Doctor after briefly sharing a house with him?

12. The Doctor tells Amy 'with regret, you're fired' in favour of which surrogate companion?

13. Which minor role was all that remained of a prospective companion, created before Catherine Tate agreed to return as Donna?

14. Which prospective companion role eventually saw light (much changed) as a part played by Ann Davies?

15. Which official is asked if he 'fancies a little excursion' to Cassiopeia, but says no?

The Tylers

1. Who does Jackie originally believe is responsible for Rose's disappearance?
2. What name does Jackie initially tell the Doctor she and Pete have given to their baby?
3. What does Jackie's friend Howard keep in his dressing gown pocket?
4. What 'ghost' does Jackie believe is visiting her?
5. What is the name of parallel-universe Jackie's dog?

6. What did parallel-universe Pete make his fortune from?
7. Who tells Elton Pope where Rose lives?
8. What does Jackie ask Elton Pope to fix for her?
9. What are Jackie's middle names?
10. Who do Jackie and Mickey save from being exterminated on the 'stolen Earth'?

*

11. On what date does Pete Tyler die?
12. What is Rose and Jackie's address on the Powell Estate?
13. Why didn't Jimbo give Rose and Jackie a lift on New Year's Day 2005?
14. Pete dies when he is hit by a car on which street?
15. According to Rose, what does Jackie watch every Bank Holiday Monday?

The Joneses

1. Who is Clive's 'trophy girlfriend'?
2. When time has been reversed after the Toclafane invasion, what is the first thing Francine wants to do?
3. Who does Tish go to work for after the death of Lazarus?
4. What does Tish tell Lazarus her perfume is called?
5. Where does Martha's cousin Adeola work?

6. Who kills Adeola?
7. What does Francine tell Martha to try to get her to visit – on Saxon's orders?
8. What Jones family event takes place on the day Martha first meets the Doctor?
9. What is Tish's job at Lazarus Laboratories?
10. What is the name of Leo's daughter?

*

11. Where is Leo at the time the rest of the Joneses are captured by the Master?
12. What did the Master force Tish, Francine and Clive to watch from the deck of the *Valiant*?
13. Martha calls Francine from the SS *Pentallian* to find the answer to what question?
14. Tish and Martha lure Lazarus to what part of Southwark Cathedral?
15. What transports Martha home to her mother during the Dalek invasion?

The Nobles

1. What is Wilf's job when he first meets the Doctor?
2. What is Donna's father's name?
3. What is Donna's married name?
4. Why can't Wilf, Sylvia and Rose communicate across the subwave network?
5. What does Wilf use to (unsuccessfully) blind a Dalek?

6. What was Wilf's army rank?
7. Why did Wilf miss Donna's wedding to Lance?
8. How does Sylvia free Wilf from his gas-filled car?
9. What group does Wilf set up to help him track down the Doctor?
10. What hobby does Wilf indulge in 'up the hill'?

11. According to Donna, what did her dad say when he got back from football?
12. Where did Wilf serve in 1948?
13. What did 6-year-old Donna do when her mum said they weren't going on holiday that year?
14. Which of Sylvia's 'Wednesday girls' takes Adipose pills?
15. Where does Donna leave her mum's car keys when she goes off in the TARDIS?

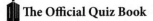

The Ponds

1. How did Amy's mother get her to like apples?
2. Who looks after young Amelia after her parents are erased from existence?
3. What is Rory's dad Brian standing on when the TARDIS materialises around him?
4. In the starless timeline, where does Amelia persuade her aunt to take her after the Doctor leaves her a message?
5. What is Amy's father's name?

6. What is the date of Amy and Rory's wedding?
7. What is Amy's mother's name?
8. What does Brian always carry with him?
9. How does Amy get her family back after Big Bang Two?
10. Where does Brian think Rory and Amy have gone travelling after their wedding?

*

11. Where are the only places Brian travels to (before he meets the Doctor), according to Rory?
12. Who does Amy accidentally marry on her and Rory's wedding anniversary?
13. How many days does Brian watch a cube, according to his log?
14. What planet does Brian send Rory and Amy a postcard from?
15. Why is Amy's father worried about his wedding speech?

The Many Lives of Clara Oswald

1. What does the Doctor call the real Clara, because of the mystery surrounding her?
2. How does the Doctor refer to Oswin?
3. What does Clara say she was born to do?
4. What are Clara's last words before jumping into the Doctor's time stream?
5. What is the Third Doctor doing when time-stream Clara spots him?

6. On what planet does time-stream Clara see the Seventh Doctor?
7. What name does Victorian Clara use as a governess?
8. On what planet does time-stream Clara see the Fourth Doctor?
9. Where is the Fifth Doctor trapped when time-stream Clara sees him?
10. What does time-stream Clara say is 'knackered' in the TARDIS she tells the First Doctor to steal?

*

11. What subject does Clara teach at Coal Hill School?
12. Who does Clara's dad tell the Doctor Clara wants to be?
13. Who are Victorian Clara's charges as governess?
14. What starliner was Oswin entertainment officer on?
15. On what date was Victorian Clara born?

The Paternoster Gang

1. What is the name of Vastra's coachman?
2. What profession does Strax adopt to serve a penance to restore the honour of his clone batch?
3. Who tries to kill Vastra after the Doctor's past is changed?
4. Who gives Strax directions to Sweetville?
5. What happens to Jenny when the Doctor's past is changed?

6. How does Vastra describe herself to Latimer's maid Alice?
7. What is the Paternoster Gang's address?
8. During the conference call with River and Clara, what does Jenny realise she forgot to do?
9. What does the Great Intelligence order the Whisper Men to do to the Paternosters and Clara unless the Doctor opens the door to his tomb?
10. Who asks Vastra to investigate the Crimson Horror?

*

11. Who offers Vastra space-time coordinates of Trenzalore in exchange for his life?
12. Where does the Doctor first meet Vastra?
13. What does Strax not enjoy as much as he'd hoped?
14. How old is Strax when he dies on Demon's Run?
15. To attack the alien snow, Strax suggests a full frontal assault with scalpel mines, acid and what else?

Companion Departures – 1960s

1. Who offers to give Susan 'a place, a time, an identity'?
2. Vicki stays in Troy to make sure who knows she didn't betray the Trojans?
3. Which two groups hope to be united under Steven's leadership when he leaves the TARDIS?
4. What machine causes Sara's death?
5. Who does Dodo send to tell the Doctor she's decided to stay behind in London?

6. Of whom does the Doctor say 'I was fond of her too, you know'?
7. What is the first thing that happens to Jamie after he is returned to his own time?
8. What is the year when Ian and Barbara return home?
9. What is the exact date Ben and Polly leave the TARDIS?
10. Who does Victoria stay with after leaving the TARDIS?

*

11. Who is the first person Zoe meets when she is returned to the Wheel?
12. What is the last thing the Doctor says to Jamie?
13. As what does the Doctor say he will always remember Katarina?
14. What does Susan discard after the Doctor leaves her on Earth?
15. What is the first place Ian sees on his return to London?

Companion Departures – 1970s

1. Where does Liz return to after leaving UNIT?
2. Where does Cliff plan that he and Jo will 'stop off' to pick up supplies and get married?
3. After leaving K-9 on Gallifrey, the Doctor produces a box labelled what?
4. Where do Cliff and Jo go for their honeymoon?
5. Where does the Doctor think he's dropped off Sarah Jane – but he hasn't?

6. What is Harry's last word on screen?
7. What tune does Sarah whistle as she walks away after the TARDIS leaves?
8. After being left in E-Space, K-9 says he has all the necessary schedules for duplicating – what?
9. What race does Romana plan to free from slavery?
10. What does the Doctor give Jo and Cliff as a wedding present?

*

11. What does the Doctor tell Andred Leela is 'terribly good' with?
12. Our last sight of which companion is an unconscious body on the floor?
13. What sort of plant does Sarah take with her on leaving the TARDIS?
14. What are the Doctor's farewell words to Romana?
15. What are Mike Yates's final on-screen words (phantasms not included)?

Companion Departures – 1980s

1. Before he leaves, who does Turlough tell to look after the Doctor?
2. Where is Tegan left behind the first time she parts company with the Doctor?
3. Who does Peri allegedly marry?
4. Who told Tegan, 'if you stop enjoying it, give it up'?
5. What substance does Nyssa aim to synthesise on Terminus?

6. According to the Matrix, who transfers Kiv's mind into Peri's body?
7. What does the Doctor use to destroy Kamelion?
8. Whose departure leads the Doctor to say he must mend his ways?
9. When Tegan worries that Nyssa will die on Terminus, Nyssa tells her that like Tegan she is – what?
10. How many logic codes does Adric have to solve to divert the freighter?

*

11. Shortly before his death, what planet does Adric say he wants to be taken to?
12. What planet does Turlough plan to return to, with Malkon?
13. How does Mel plan to send the Doctor a postcard?
14. What spaceship does Mel plan to travel in?
15. Whose last words are 'Hey! What do you want –'?

Companion Departures – 2005 onwards

1. What does the Doctor say will happen to Donna if she remembers him?
2. Who writes the afterword in Melody Malone's book?
3. Who saves Rose from being sucked into the Void?
4. What does Martha give the Doctor before the TARDIS leaves without her?
5. What does Rory spot just before he disappears?

6. Why hasn't the Doctor ever acknowledged the echo of River?
7. Who manipulates the timelines to help Donna become the DoctorDonna?
8. What does Rose hold to stop herself being drawn into the Void?
9. Who does Martha phone before saying goodbye to the Doctor?
10. How old is Amy when she dies?

*

11. What does the Doctor say will happen if they try to rescue Angel-zapped Rory in the TARDIS?
12. What are Amy's last words to the Doctor (in person)?
13. Why hasn't River's echo faded by the time the Doctor goes to Trenzalore?
14. From what does the Doctor get enough power to contact Rose in Bad Wolf Bay?
15. Which two kings does the Doctor suggest taking Martha to see, before she tells him she's not going with him?

Closing Credits

Initially – D

1. What D is the creator of the Daleks?
2. What D is the sound the Master hears constantly?
3. What D are female warriors who come from Galaxy 4?
4. What D is a sort of seal that the sonic screwdriver can't unlock?
5. What D is the planet the Dominators plan to destroy to fuel their ships?

6. What D is American tourist Morton?
7. What D is an offensive term for Draconian?
8. What D is the village duplicated by the Kraals?
9. What D is the weapon developed on Uxarieus?
10. What D is the Kroton machine that needs high brains?

11. What D is a pirate who fights Amy Pond?
12. What D is the surname adopted by Dodo in the Wild West?
13. What D is a G-class planet in Tau Ceti?
14. What D is the secret of life, revealed to the Doctor by a hermit?
15. What D does Harrison Chase order Scorby to 'get'?

Initially – E

1. What E is worn by Madame Kovarian and Guy Crayford?
2. What E is a planet covered with cloud banks full of fish?
3. What E serves the Jagrafess on Satellite Five?
4. What E does the Fourth Doctor claim he walks in?
5. What E is the final word of the incantation used to defeat the Carrionites?

6. What E is one of Omega's 'less successful attempts at psychosynthesis'?
7. What E is the Tythonian ambassador to Chloris?
8. What E is a planet containing a living city that is visited by the Third Doctor and the Daleks?
9. What E is a Kastrian, whose hand survived execution?
10. What E is Greek for 'this bath's too hot', according to the Fourth Doctor?

*

11. What E is the leader of the Silurians who live below Cwmtaff?
12. What E is the name the Eternals give to those who dwell in time?
13. What E is the wife of Edward of Wessex?
14. What E is the yellow Dalek of the Dalek Paradigm?
15. What E is the home planet of the Mandrels?

Initially – F

1. What F is the Rock where the Doctor meets a Rutan?
2. What F is the jewel that Christoper gave to Lady Edison?
3. What 'F' was the secret that the ancient tribe encountered by the First Doctor had lost?
4. What F is Helen A's pet?
5. What F, along with a core, makes up a Fendahl?

6. What F became a food taster 'because she was hungry'?
7. What F are the sharp-toothed savages on Malcaissaro?
8. What F do most of the work on Inter Minor?
9. What F is evil from the dawn of time?
10. What F is Captain Avery's ship?

11. What F is a Gallfreyan insect whose lifecycle was studied by Romana?
12. What F is a beautiful planet with 'sands as soft as swan's down'?
13. What F would Romana have preferred to be called by the Doctor?
14. What F is a canned drink found in Paradise Towers?
15. What F is the maid who helps the Doctor and Rose fight werewolves?

Opening Titles (2)

Initially – G

1. What G is the robot on Bowie Base One?
2. What G is the station that was once Satellite Five?
3. What G are gaseous beings who ask to be pitied?
4. What G is used to control weather from the Moon?
5. What G is there 'nothing only' about being, according to Sarah Jane?

6. What G are the sluglike aliens led by Mestor?
7. What G is queen of Atlantis?
8. What G is the leader of the Bannermen?
9. What G is a fictional character who aids the Doctor in the Land of Fiction?
10. What G is a coward whose biggest fear is the Weeping Angels?

11. What G is the count who planned to marry Romana?
12. What G is Pete Tyler's codename when he gives information to the Preachers?
13. What G is Hade, who works for the Company?
14. What G is the duke who is nephew of Count Federico?
15. What G is one of the Cybermen at the South Pole?

Initially – H

1. What H is the archer who serves Edward of Wessex?
2. What H is Yvonne, CEO of the Torchwood Institute?
3. What H is the shop where Rose works?
4. What H feeds on artron energy and lures Time Lords to the rift where it lives?
5. What H is the comet the Cyberman plan to use to destroy Earth?

6. What H is Binro, who believes there are other suns and other worlds?
7. What H is a theoretical absurdity, according to the Doctor and Romana?
8. What H is the novice who tends to the Face of Boe as her punishment for past misdeeds?
9. What H is the Sixth Doctor's nickname for Humker?
10. What H is the astrologer who leads the Brotherhood of Demnos?

*

11. What H is the colour worn by the Patrexes on Gallifrey?
12. What H is the month that comes before Pandoff in the Pan Traffic calendar?
13. What H is the alien the Doctor and Rose are pursuing at the time they meet Elton Pope?
14. What H is the surname of fictional character Captain Jack?
15. What H is the professor who excavates Devil's Hump?

Initially – I

1. What I is The Doctor's Wife?
2. What I teaches science at Coal Hill School?
3. What I is the gate that is really a Vinvocci healing device?
4. What I loves Chloe Webber?
5. What I is Winston Churchill's name for the Daleks?

6. What I christens Linx the 'star warrior' and 'Toadface'?
7. What I is the country where Lady Eddison met Christopher?
8. What I is a space trading colony on the dark side of Svartos?
9. What I is the galaxy where Vortis and the Face of Boe can be found?
10. What I backfires, making Jackson Lake believe he is the Doctor?

11. What I is the Aztec warrior who fought Ian?
12. What I is the sole survivor of the Silurian Triad?
13. What I is used to hold back glaciers (and defeat the Ice Warriors)?
14. What I is Guido's daughter, sent to the Calvierri school?
15. What I does Turlough nickname 'Hippo'?

Episode Two
Adventures in Time and Space

Time Travel – Past

Match each story with the year it is (mainly) set in:

1.	*The Time Meddler*	1794
2.	*The Romans*	1869
3.	*The Visitation*	1289
4.	*The Empty Child*	1572
5.	*The Reign of Terror*	1851
6.	*The King's Demons*	1883
7.	*Black Orchid*	1881
8.	*Delta and the Bannermen*	64
9.	*Marco Polo*	1925
10.	*The Massacre*	1959
11.	*Pyramids of Mars*	1666
12.	*The Next Doctor*	1215
13.	*Ghost Light*	1941
14.	*The Gunfighters*	1066
15.	*The Unquiet Dead*	1911

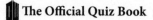

Time Travel – Present (or is it?)

Match each story with the year it is (mainly) set in. These stories took place during the *Doctor Who* era (i.e. 1963–present) – but some may have been either future or historical stories at the time of broadcast…

1.	*Mawdryn Undead* (earlier time zone)	2006
2.	*Remembrance of the Daleks*	1988
3.	*Doctor Who* (TV movie)	2005
4.	*Rose*	1987
5.	*Fear Her*	1999
6.	*Aliens of London*	1979
7.	*Logopolis*	1986
8.	*City of Death*	2012
9.	*Silver Nemesis*	1981
10.	*The Awakening*	1977
11.	*The Faceless Ones*	1984
12.	*The Tenth Planet*	1983
13.	*Hide*	1966
14.	*Father's Day*	1963
15.	*Cold War*	1974

Time Travel – Future

Match each story with the year it is (mainly) set in:

1.	*The Daleks' Master Plan*	2018
2.	*The Invisible Enemy*	5,000,000,000
3.	*The End of the World*	4000
4.	*New Earth*	2070
5.	*Gridlock*	2116
6.	*The Moonbase*	2472
7.	*Planet of Evil*	5,000,000,053
8.	*The Enemy of the World*	2526
9.	*Warriors of the Deep*	5,000,000,023
10.	*Colony in Space*	2986
11.	*Earthshock*	5000
12.	*Dinosaurs on a Spaceship*	37,166
13.	*Terror of the Vervoids*	2084
14.	*The Leisure Hive*	2367
15.	*Nightmare of Eden*	2290

Name-Dropping

Which Doctor encountered – or claimed to have encountered – the following historical figures?

1. Richard Nixon
2. Louis XV
3. Puccini
4. Nero
5. Richard the Lionheart

6. The Venerable Bede
7. Admiral Nelson
8. William Tell
9. Marie Antoinette
10. Pablo Picasso

11. Bing Crosby
12. Hypatia
13. Dame Nellie Melba
14. Pyrrho
15. Emmeline Pankhurst

Planet-Hopping

Which planets are these?

1. Earth's twin planet, home to the Cybermen.
2. Planet where the Cybermen built their ice tombs, home of the Cryons.
3. The Tenth Doctor takes a trip across this diamond planet which has a sapphire waterfall.
4. Nyssa's home planet.
5. Land of the Kinda.

6. Planet where the Doctor and Ace visit the Psychic Circus.
7. Twin planets on the edge of the helical galaxy, visited by the Doctor during his search for the Key to Time.
8. Home of the Abzorbaloff, twin planet of Raxacoricofallapatorius.
9. The planet of the dead in the Scorpion Nebula, once home to a population of one hundred billion.
10. Planet forced to pay tribute to Skonnos.

*

11. The Ninth Doctor wanted to take Rose to this planet, where the dogs had no noses.
12. According to the Third Doctor, the natives of this planet communicate with their eyebrows.
13. Planet on which the Doctor and Rose visit a beach a thousand miles long and walk under frozen waves a hundred feet tall.
14. The seventh planet of the Dundra system, home of the Aplan maze of the dead.
15. World beyond Alpha Geminorum, promised to Luke Rattigan by the Sontarans.

Could You Say That Again?

1. In the language of the Gamma Forest, how does 'Melody Pond' translate?
2. On Traken, what monster name means 'a fly trapped in honey'?
3. What phrase is carved on the oldest rock face in history, revealed by the TARDIS translation circuits?
4. Where do the Doctor and Rose find writing that is so old the TARDIS can't translate it?
5. Blon Fel-Fotch plans to build the Blaidd Drwg power station in Cardiff – what does its name mean in English?

6. When Martha is searching for the Osterhagen key, what language does she hear the Daleks using?
7. The Master often chooses aliases that are translations of Master. What names does he adopt that are (a) Latin and (b) Greek?
8. 'Silence will fall' is the usual translation of a prophecy regarding Trenzalore – what does Dorium say would be a better translation?
9. In the language of the Gamma Forest, what word means 'Mighty Warrior'?
10. The Second Doctor once called himself by what name that means 'Doctor of Who' in German?

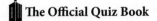

11. What does the name of the Norwegian beach 'Dårlig ulv stranden' mean in English?
12. From the scriptures of the Veltino, what does the name 'Krop Tor' mean in English?
13. What monster name literally means 'the shadows that melt the flesh'?
14. Whose grandfather translated the Viking inscriptions found in St Jude's crypt?
15. Who was surprised that the TARDIS could translate 'even French'?

The Real World

Sometimes programmes from the real world pop up in *Doctor Who* – and real people from our world too. In which story or stories can you find:

1. The Master watching *The Clangers*?
2. The Master watching *Teletubbies*?
3. A special edition of *EastEnders*?
4. A special edition of *Blue Peter*?
5. McFly endorsing a political candidate?

6. Patrick Moore via video conferencing?
7. Courtney Pine playing jazz?
8. Brian Cox being interviewed on the news?
9. A member of Torchwood watching Paul O'Grady?
10. Andrew Marr reporting on the political situation?

11. The Doctor watching *Tommy Zoom*?
12. A special edition of *The Apprentice*?
13. Kenneth Kendall reading the news?
14. Presenter Alex Macintosh reporting on a peace conference?
15. The cartoon *Pedro and Frankensheep*?

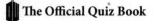

Inspector Gadget

In which story do we first come across:

1. The Chameleon Arch?
2. The Hand of Omega?
3. The sonic screwdriver?
4. The Doctor's recorder?
5. The randomiser?

6. The TARDIS fault locator?
7. The laser screwdriver?
8. Nitro 9?
9. The psychic paper?
10. The TARDIS food machine?

11. Bessie?
12. The cloister bell?
13. Jelly babies?
14. The space-time telegraph?
15. Hallucinogenic lipstick?

Never Seen Again

Some abilities or possessions of the Doctor's pop up to do a specific job – but no matter how useful they seem, he never produces them again. In what story do we see:

1. TARDIS authorised control disc?
2. Sonic cane?
3. Time Scanner?
4. Special Straw?
5. Time and Space Visualiser

6. Bessie's anti-theft device?
7. Bessie's super-drive?
8. Bessie's remote control?
9. TARDIS log?
10. TARDIS pause control?

11. Magnetic Chair?
12. Astral Map?
13. Records of Rassilon?
14. Time Logs?
15. TARDIS seatbelts?

I Cross the Void Beyond the Mind...

The Doctor uses his TARDIS to travel through time and space, but it's not the only transport available...

1. What does Borusa use to bring various Doctors and companions to the Death Zone on Gallifrey?
2. Who use a Dalek time ship to return to their own place and time?
3. What does a Time Lord give to the Doctor to return him to the TARDIS after he's completed his mission on Skaro?
4. Who is caught up by a time storm in her bedroom that takes her to another time and place?
5. Who is the first person to teleport using Project Indigo?

6. According to legend, what creatures guided the early space travellers through the asteroid belts?
7. Who creates a time contour to try to escape from prehistoric Earth?
8. Maxtible and Waterfield's successful time experiments use mirrors and what sort of electricity?
9. The development of what sort of transport systems in the twenty-first century led to rockets being consigned to museums?

10. What did Arbitan give to the TARDIS crew to transport them around Marinus?

11. What device, usually worn on the wrist, is used by Time Agents to travel through time?

12. What connects the planet Karfel to Scotland?

13. What animals are transported to Mira by molecular dissemination, along with the Doctor, Steven and Sara?

14. What time sensitives are forced to navigate human ships through the time winds?

15. Who invented hyposlip travel systems?

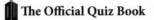
Writerly Riddles 1 – Shakespeare

1. In which story do the First Doctor and friends watch Shakespeare meeting with Elizabeth I?
2. Which companion comes to share a name with an eponymous Shakespearean character?
3. The story title *The Shakespeare Code* is a play on the name of what book and film?
4. In *The Shakespeare Code*, Shakespeare promises a sequel to which play?
5. Who is revealed to be Shakespeare's 'Dark Lady'?

6. Which friend of the Sixth Doctor says as he lies dying: 'No one will ever see my definitive Hamlet now'?
7. The name of which monster does Shakespeare take from the Tenth Doctor to use in a play?
8. What caused Shakespeare's madness that allowed the Carrionites to gain entrance?
9. The Fourth Doctor claims to have written out the first draft of which Shakespeare play?
10. What proves to the Tenth Doctor that Shakespeare is a genius?

*

11. Which of these phrases does the Tenth Doctor *not* give to Shakespeare: (a) 'All the world's a stage', (b) 'Once more unto the breach' or (c) 'The play's the thing'?

12. In which story does the Doctor quote Shakespeare and say he was a 'Charming Fellow. Dreadful actor'?

13. The costumes for which Fourth Doctor story had previously been used in a 1954 film of *Romeo and Juliet*?

14. What play idea do the TARDIS crew witness Elizabeth I give to Shakespeare?

15. Which Doctor says of Shakespeare, 'Interesting fellow, the Bard. Must see him again some time'?

Writerly Riddles 2 – Agatha Christie

1. What Agatha Christie book is Professor Lasky seen reading in *Terror of the Vervoids*?
2. BBC Radio's Miss Marple, June Whitfield, played which character in *Doctor Who*?
3. Which *Doctor Who* scriptwriter has also written several scripts for Agatha Christie's *Poirot* (ITV)?
4. Who gives Agatha the idea for Miss Marple?
5. According to the Tenth Doctor, how many times have Agatha Christie's plots fooled him?

6. What is Lady Eddison's favourite Agatha Christie book?
7. In which story does the Tenth Doctor tell Martha that he wants to meet Agatha Christie?
8. Which of these Agatha Christie titles is not referenced in *The Unicorn and the Wasp*: (a) *Hickory Dickory Dock*, (b) *Sparkling Cyanide* or (c) *Crooked House*?
9. What traumatic event had happened to Agatha just before the Eddison's house party?
10. A giant wasp – like a Vespiform – is featured on the cover of which book, that the Doctor shows Donna?

*

11. What clue does Agatha discover in Lady Eddison's sitting room?
12. What reason does Agatha Christie give for making her detective Belgian?
13. Which of these Doctors has not (as of 2013) appeared in an Agatha Christie television production: Tom Baker, Peter Davison, Colin Baker, Paul McGann, Christopher Eccleston or Peter Capaldi?
14. Hugh Fraser, ITV's Captain Hastings, made his television debut as an uncredited extra in which *Doctor Who* story?
15. In what year did Agatha Christie disappear (both in real life and in *Doctor Who*)?

Writerly Riddles 3 – Charles Dickens

1. Who is so excited about seeing Dickens that she attends his reading despite being dead?
2. On what date do the Doctor and Rose first meet Dickens?
3. Which of his works is Dickens reading to the theatre audience just before Rose and the Doctor enter?
4. According to the Doctor, for how long do Dickens's books last?
5. What do the ladies call Dickens, according to the Doctor?

6. What work of Dickens does the Doctor say is the best short story ever written?
7. What part of a Dickens work does the Doctor suspect was 'just padding'?
8. What part of a Dickens work does the Doctor say 'cracks him up'?
9. Which of these works is not namechecked by the Doctor when he meets Dickens: *Bleak House*, *Oliver Twist* or *Hard Times*?
10. What Dickens hero does the Sixth Doctor quote in *The Ultimate Foe*?

*

11. What does Dickens suggest as a new title for his final work?
12. At what Cardiff theatre does Dickens do his reading?
13. In an alternative timeline, who interviews Dickens on television about his new 'Christmas special'?
14. Which of these Doctor actors has not (as of 2013) appeared in a screen adaptation of Dickens's work: William Hartnell, Patrick Troughton or Peter Capaldi?
15. Which Doctor actor played the role of Eugene Wrayburn in a screen adaptation of *Our Mutual Friend*?

True or False 1 – Metals and Minerals

Which of these metals or minerals are mentioned in the television series, and which are made up? (One of the answers is a genuine substance – a bonus point if you can identify it!)

1. Dalekanium
2. Tarylium
3. Dwarf-star alloy
4. Argonite
5. Cybron

6. Essentite
7. Jethrik
8. Validium
9. Owlenium
10. Molybdenum

11. Phelatite
12. Bazoolium
13. Naimisk
14. Hymetusite
15. Jasonite

True or False 2 – TARDIS Bits

Which of these TARDIS components or tools are mentioned in the television series, and which are made up?

1. Phase deflector
2. Chameleon Circuit
3. Radiation blocker
4. Space wrench
5. Fluid link

6. Mergin nut
7. Comparator
8. Temporal limiter
9. Chrono-controls
10. Ferris claw

11. Ganymede driver
12. Andromeda spanner
13. Cat's eye nebuliser
14. Atom accelerator
15. Dimensional stabiliser

True or False 3 – Planets

Which of these planets are mentioned in the television series, and which are made up?

1. Florana
2. Bessan
3. Marn
4. Gundan
5. Tigus

6. Exodus
7. Felspoon
8. Astrala Major
9. Terra Omega
10. Kurhan

11. Granados
12. Sinda Callista
13. Messaline Majoria
14. Shallacatop
15. Bonsarn Ferana

True or False 4 – UNIT Personnel

Which of these UNIT soldiers are mentioned in the television series, and which are made up?

1. Private Wyatt
2. Private Harris
3. Captain Magambo
4. Corporal Cooke
5. Private Stanley

6. Private Perkins
7. Lieutenant Richards
8. Corporal Cole
9. Captain Spokes
10. Sergeant Houghton

11. Sergeant Lyons
12. Corporal Tracy
13. Corporal Champion
14. Corporal Forbes
15. Private Bryson

Time Lord Biology

1. How long can the Fifth Doctor survive in sub-zero temperatures?
2. What aspect of Time Lord biology helps the Doctor survive a mummy attack?
3. What skill did Romana learn at school that enables her to escape from a Dalek slave gang?
4. What does the Doctor tell Ralph Cornish he can withstand considerably more of than most people?
5. Which Doctor claims that he might have two heads, or no head, after regenerating?

6. What is the first story to mention that the Doctor has two hearts?
7. In what story does Ian say of the Doctor 'his heart seems all right and his breathing's quite regular'?
8. After absorbing a huge amount of Roentgen radiation, how does the Tenth Doctor expel it?
9. What can the Fifth Doctor store for several minutes, helping him to reach the Queen Bat on Androzani Minor?
10. Lapsing into a coma before arrival on Spiridon, the Third Doctor's hearts beat approximately how often?

11. What rate does the Third Doctor's pulse 'settle down' to while in Ashbridge Cottage Hospital?
12. What is the 'more or less normal' rate of the Third Doctor's pulse after he returns from the alternative Earth?
13. What can Dastari isolate from a Time Lord's body that's needed to control the TARDIS?
14. According to Dr Lomax, what shows that the Third Doctor's blood is not a human type?
15. What is the Seventh Doctor's fibrillation rate according to Dr Salinger?

Family and Early Life

1. Who is the Doctor's granddaughter?
2. According to the Eighth Doctor, what race was his mother?
3. In which story does the Doctor say of his family, 'But when they died, that part of me died with them. It'll never come back. Not now'?
4. Whose father had pastures on the slopes of Mount Perdition where the Doctor used to run all day?
5. At what age was the Doctor taken from his family to join the Academy?

6. What did the young Doctor do after looking into the Untempered Schism?
7. In which story does the Doctor tell Rose, 'I was a dad once'?
8. In which story does the Doctor say that his family 'sleep in his mind'?
9. According to the Rani, what was the Doctor's specialist subject at university?
10. Who does the Third Doctor finally recognise as having been his teacher and guru in 'another time, another place'?

*

11. What does Amy say is hanging above the Doctor's cot?
12. Who asks the Doctor if he has any family, to which he replies, 'I don't know'?
13. What does the Doctor reply when Martha asks if he has a brother?
14. What does the Doctor reply when Martha says of the Master, 'I thought you were going to say he was your secret brother or something'?
15. What does the Eighth Doctor remember watching with his father on a warm Gallifreyan night?

Fruit 'n' Veg

1. What vegetable does the Fifth Doctor wear on his lapel?
2. The Vespiform's first victim shares a name with which fruit?
3. Who did the Doctor once share a cell with in the Tower of London, who kept going on about a vegetable he'd discovered called the potato?
4. What fruit does the Fourth Doctor claim to have dropped onto Isaac Newton's head?
5. What fruit does Sarah pluck from a tree to eat in fifteenth-century Italy?

6. Eating what vegetable exposes Andy Stone to the Flood?
7. What fruit, thanks to the Doctor, grows on Villengard where there were once weapon factories?
8. What fruit does the Doctor use to defeat the Sycorax Leader?
9. As well as pickled onions, what other pickled vegetable could be found in Mickey Smith's kitchen?
10. What does the Eleventh Doctor suggest could be grown in the Silurians' base?

*

11. What fruit is the First Doctor seen munching in *The Five Doctors?*
12. What fruit does the First Doctor delightedly spot in Morphoton?
13. Who won't eat lemon juice, lime, grapefruit, orange or avocado?
14. Which rebellious scientist lives in a plant museum containing tomatoes, carrots, potatoes and strawberries?
15. Tom Baker famously wanted a talking version of which vegetable as a companion?

Bookworms

1. What is the subject of Amy's favourite book as a child?
2. Who is the real author of the Doctor's book about Melody Malone, private detective?
3. At the start of which story is the Eleventh Doctor seen reading a book on advanced quantum mechanics?
4. Where can be found 'whole continents of Jeffrey Archer, Bridget Jones, Monty Python's Big Red Book'?
5. What is the subject of the book Barbara lends to Susan in *An Unearthly Child*?

6. What children's book is K-9 reading at the beginning of *The Creature from the Pit*?
7. What book is being read by Artie in *The Bells of Saint John*?
8. In which story is Ian seen reading *Monsters from Outer Space* (which he says is 'a bit far-fetched')?
9. What is the title of George Cranleigh's book about his travels?
10. What is the title of the final chapter in Melody Malone's book?

*

11. Who is the author of *A Journal of Impossible Things*, based on Joan Redfern's life?
12. What book does the Fourth Doctor produce to help himself read *Everest in Easy Stages*?
13. What book does Jamie hear an extract from when he switches on a machine in the Land of Fiction?
14. In which story is the Fourth Doctor seen reading *Origins of the Universe* by Oolon Colluphid?
15. What book hangs from the TARDIS ceiling in *The Greatest Show in the Galaxy*?

Music to My Ears

In which *Doctor Who* stories as broadcast (not necessarily on the DVD versions) do we hear the following songs:

1. 'Mr Blue Sky' – ELO
2. 'I Can't Decide' – The Scissor Sisters
3. 'The Birdie Song' – The Tweets
4. 'Ticket To Ride' – The Beatles
5. 'Tainted Love' – Soft Cell

6. 'Never Gonna Give You Up' – Rick Astley
7. 'The Lion Sleeps Tonight' – Tight Fit
8. 'Starman' – David Bowie
9. 'Ghost Town' – The Specials
10. 'Twenty-Four Hours From Tulsa' – Gene Pitney

11. 'In a Dream' – Pat Hodge
12. 'Teddy Bears Picnic'
13. 'Paperback Writer' – The Beatles
14. 'Oh Well' – Fleetwood Mac
15. 'A Whiter Shade of Pale' – Procul Harum

UNIT Good Guys

1. Which 'technical fellow' works on a machine to get through the heat barrier around Devil's End?
2. Which scientific adviser does the Doctor call his 'new best friend'?
3. Which officer is killed by a Silurian after saving the Brigadier's life?
4. Who is Isobel Watkins's 'dolly soldier'?
5. Which female soldier assists the Brigadier during the First World Peace Conference and the Axon invasion?

6. Which officer reports the discovery of the newly regenerated Third Doctor unconscious beside the TARDIS?
7. Which sergeant serves under both Brigadiers Lethbridge-Stewart and Bambera?
8. Who from the Scientific Supplies Section is a 'dolly Scotsman', according to Jo?
9. Which unfortunate soldier is turned into compost by Harrison Chase?
10. The Doctor objects to Luke Rattigan calling which soldier 'a grunt'?

*

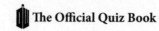

11. Which officer kills Commander Skorr and is kissed by a UNIT captain?
12. Who sends the *Gallifrey Falls* painting to the Black Archives at the Doctor's request?
13. Which soldier gives Bok 'five rounds rapid'?
14. Which 'warrior maid' is killed by Morgaine?
15. Which officer is turned into a skeleton onboard the Sycorax ship?

Christmas Conundrums 1

1. What Christmas song is played by the Tylers' deadly Christmas tree?
2. What annual Christmas event is cancelled due to the Sycorax invasion?
3. Which of these original songs is not first heard in a Christmas episode: (a) 'My Angel Put The Devil In Me' (b) 'Love Don't Roam' (c) 'Song For Ten'?
4. According to Mr Copper, who do humans worship?
5. Who does Sardick call 'Little Miss Christmas'?

6. The episode 'The Feast of Steven' (*The Daleks' Master Plan* episode 7) was broadcast on Christmas Day in which year?
7. After the defeat of the Gelth, why does Charles Dickens catch the mail coach to London?
8. What does the Master refer to as 'The Christmas star that came to kill'?
9. According to the Doctor, who got 'the last room' at the first Christmas?
10. In *The End of Time, Part One*, what book does Donna give Wilf for Christmas?

*

11. Where does the Ninth Doctor think he is when the TARDIS arrives in Cardiff on Christmas Eve?

12. What colour paper hat does Rose get out of her Christmas cracker?

13. What colour bicycle did Father Christmas – or possibly the Doctor – give Rose when she was 12?

14. What does the Doctor use to blow a hole in the wall of the tunnel below HC Clements?

15. Jackson Lake invites the Doctor to a Christmas feast at what establishment?

Christmas Conundrums 2

1. What first attracts the Robot Santa Pilot Fish to the Doctor?
2. According to the Doctor, what's always tucked away at the bottom of the presents?
3. On what date was Donna's wedding to Lance held: (a) 23 December, (b) 24 December or (c) 26 December?
4. Who sacrifices herself to prevent Max Capricorn's 'Christmas inferno'?
5. What is the Doctor's infamous toast at the end of 'The Feast of Steven'?

6. *In The End of Time, Part One*, what does Wilf say would make his Christmas?
7. What Christmas character does Sarah liken the Doctor to after their arrival on Skaro?
8. What one-word message does Victorian Clara send to get the Doctor to help her?
9. According to Mr Copper, who do the people of UK go to war with every Christmas Eve?
10. Who are reportedly the only people who've stayed in London for Christmas following two previous Christmas attacks?

11. For whom is Clara cooking Christmas dinner when she asks the Doctor to pretend to be her boyfriend?
12. What carol is being played by a band before Wilf enters the church in *The End of Time, Part One*?
13. What did the first settlers on Sardick's world call Christmas?
14. What does the Eleventh Doctor call Father Christmas?
15. What Christmas carol are the policemen singing at the beginning of The Feast of Steven?

Till Death Us Do Part

1. What is Jackie and Pete's wedding present for Sarah and Stuart?
2. What famous film star does the Doctor apparently marry?
3. Who wants to create an interplanetary alliance with Earth by marrying Jo Grant?
4. How does the First Doctor become engaged to Cameca?
5. Which Doctor says, 'I'm rubbish at weddings, especially my own'?

6. What represents 'something old, something new, something borrowed, something blue' at Amy and Rory's wedding?
7. To whom does Richard the Lionheart plan to marry his sister?
8. According to Prince Reynart, what will almost certainly happen to Romana five minutes after she marries him?
9. Who does the Doctor borrow a pound from to buy a wedding present for Donna?
10. What does River Song say the Doctor always does at weddings?

*

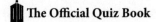

11. Who plans to catch the bouquet at Donna and Shaun's wedding?
12. What joins the Doctor's hand to River's at their marriage?
13. Where is Donna's wedding to Lance being held?
14. How many Doctors are present at the Tenth Doctor's wedding to Elizabeth I?
15. What happens to Ping-Cho's intended husband?

Are You Qualified?

1. Which Doctor claims he gained his medical degree in 1888 under Lister?
2. Which companion failed her general science A level?
3. Which close friend of the Doctor's is a professor of archaeology?
4. Which companion got suspended from school while studying for her chemistry A level?
5. Which friend of the Doctor's is a biologist with a Nobel prize?

6. Which companion does the Brigadier describe as an expert in meteorites with degrees 'in medicine, physics and a dozen other subjects'?
7. Which acquaintance of the Doctor has a degree in Earthonomics?
8. Which companion left school because of Jimmy Stone?
9. Which companion is an astrophysicist, pure mathematics major (with honours)?
10. Which Doctor describes himself as a doctor of 'practically everything'?

*

11. In which subject did the Master get a higher class of degree than the Doctor?
12. Which companion wants to learn graphology?
13. Which Doctor claims to have degrees in medicine and cheese-making?
14. Which acquaintance of the Doctor's is a professor who specialises in extraterrestrial pathological endomorphisms?
15. Which companion earned a certificate of education in medicine, physics and chemistry at the age of ten?

Leave Me, Doctor! Save Yourself!

1. Who ejects herself and her sun-possessed husband out of an airlock on the SS *Pentallian*?
2. What is the job of the woman who sacrifices herself to save the Doctor from the entity on Midnight?
3. Who deliberately runs in front of a car to save the world from the Reapers?
4. Who steps in front of a lorry so her past self will turn left?
5. Who ejects herself and Kirksen out of an airlock on the Spar?

6. Who blows up himself and the vampirised Venetian girls with gunpowder?
7. Who pushes the Second Doctor out of the way of a Dalek's weapon on Skaro?
8. Who deliberately sets off a booby trap on Voga, killing himself and two Cybermen?
9. Who says the Doctor 'knew him at his best' as he is about to be killed by Weeping Angels?
10. Who swaps places with the Doctor to set off the atmospheric converter and destroy the Sontarans?

*

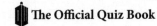

11. Who pilots a spaceship off Uxarieus to save his fellow colonists?
12. Who cuts the last synestic lock on the Space Ark's transport ship?
13. Who blows up a Dalek ship and himself above Exxilon?
14. Which Moon-based Ice Warrior collaborator betrays their plans to Earth although it means his death when caught?
15. Who cuts a rope so he won't drag Ian to his death?

Planetary Puzzles 1 – Skaro

1. According to the title of the first episode of *The Daleks*, what is Skaro?
2. What does the Seventh Doctor use to destroy Skaro?
3. What planet does the Cult of Skaro plan to transform into New Skaro?
4. Who, according to the Eighth Doctor, was finally put on trial on Skaro?
5. The First Doctor tricks his companions into staying on Skaro so he can visit which feature?

6. What part-animal, part-vegetable organism is native to Skaro?
7. After *The Daleks*, which is the next story to see the Doctor visiting Skaro?
8. According to Alydon, how long was 'the final war' on Skaro?
9. What did the Doctor and his friends first believe had created the petrified forest?
10. What part of Skaro is home to the Mutos?

*

11. What metal creature is found in Skaro's petrified forest?
12. Who lures the Eleventh Doctor to Skaro?
13. Skaro is which numbered planet in its solar system?
14. How is Skaro listed in the Movellan's star catalogue?
15. Which Thal is killed while filling water bags at the Lake of Mutations?

Planetary Puzzles 2 – New Earth

1. What is the name of the order of cat nuns in charge of the hospital?
2. What creatures are found in the fast lane?
3. What sort of grass is found on New Earth?
4. Whose message brings the Doctor and Rose to New Earth?
5. What holographic character provides traffic news for those stuck on the motorway?

6. How many people are there in New New York City at the time of the Doctor and Rose's visit?
7. How many years pass on New Earth between the Doctor's two visits?
8. In what district of the undercity do the Doctor and Martha arrive?
9. The population of New Earth are killed by a virus mutating inside which new mood?
10. How long does it take for the virus to wipe everyone out?

*

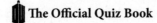

11. Where did Valerie and Brannigan start their trip?
12. Where are Milo and Cheen heading for, where they think they'll find blue sky and houses made of wood?
13. What does Martha think the undercity looks like?
14. For how long is the planet automatically quarantined?
15. How many New Yorks have there been since the original on Earth?

Planetary Puzzles 3 – The Solar System

1. Who is Guardian of the Solar System in the year 4000?
2. What is the 'thirteenth moon' of Jupiter, visited by the Fourth Doctor?
3. What city on Pluto is visited by the Fourth Doctor?
4. Which of Saturn's moons does the Doctor visit in 5000?
5. Which planet of the solar system has metal seas, according to Susan?

6. Who use the planets of the solar system as marker buoys in their race?
7. What is the only planet on which Taranium can be found?
8. What does the Doctor suspect the Ice Warriors used their 'might and wisdom' to freeze on Mars?
9. What planet is *Guinevere One* heading for before it is hijacked by the Sycorax?
10. According to the Doctor, how long does it take radio waves to pass from Mars to Earth?

*

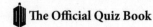

11. A stabiliser failure sent Guy Crayford's ship into orbit around which planet – or so he told Earth?
12. Bowie Base One is built in which Mars crater?
13. According to K-9, what is the outermost body in the solar system?
14. What is the penal planet of the Solar System in the year 4000?
15. How many people are there in the Solar System as of the year 4000?

Planetary Puzzles 4 – Peladon

1. What planet did King Peladon's mother come from?
2. Who is able to confirm the Doctor's identity on his second trip to Peladon?
3. Who is High Priest at the time of the Doctor's first visit to Peladon?
4. Who is Chancellor at the time of the Doctor's second visit to Peladon?
5. What is the royal emblem of Peladon?

6. Who are the only people who may set foot in the throne room?
7. Under what title is Jo introduced to King Peladon?
8. Who is King Peladon's champion?
9. Which Federation delegate tries to prevent Peladon joining the Federation?
10. Where is the Aggedor beast kept at the time of the Doctor's first visit to Peladon?

*

11. Who does the Doctor think was behind his landing on Peladon at a moment of crisis?
12. What rare mineral is found on Peladon?
13. How much time passes on Peladon between the Doctor's first and second visits?
14. Who does the Doctor suggest should be Queen Thalira's new Chancellor?
15. Ettis hides the sonic lance in a cave on what mountain?

We've Got Your Number 1

Fill in the missing numerals:

1. K-_ – the Doctor's robot dog
2. L_ – maintenance robot Drathro
3. WHO _ – Bessie's numberplate
4. Type __ – the type of TARDIS used by the Doctor
5. SV_ – Deadly Super-Voc on the Sandminer

6. Warehouse __ – where the Ood brain is kept
7. Mars Probe _ – British spaceship crewed by Lefee and Michaels
8. P_E – spaceship containing the Minyan race banks
9. Zeiton _ – essential TARDIS fuel found on Varos
10. Adipose _ – Adipose breeding planet that went missing

*

11. DN_ – pesticide that poisons Barbara Wright
12. Sleep __ – mood drug used on Martha by Cheen
13. Toll port G___ – port where the Seventh Doctor won a trip to 1950s Earth
14. Crusader __ – space truck that takes the Tenth Doctor across Midnight
15. Mustakozene __ – chemical that caused Megelen to merge with a Morlox

We've Got Your Number 2

Fill in the missing numerals:

1. W_ – the Wheel in Space
2. Sea Base _ – base attacked by Silurians and Sea Devils
3. Galaxy _ – home of the Drahvins
4. __ Totter's Lane – the TARDIS's first landing place
5. Galaxy _ – galaxy at war with the Galactic Federation

6. R_C – Minyan spaceship searching for the race banks
7. Sanctuary Base _ – base on Krop Tor visited by the Doctor and Rose
8. Windmill ___ – UNIT helicopter searching for Silurians
9. Chameleon ___ – Chameleon Tours flight to Rome, boarded by Jamie
10. J__ – one of the codes required for bacon and eggs from the TARDIS food machine

*

11. RA_____ – Urbanka's home galaxy
12. ___ Squadron – Captain Jack Harkness's RAF squadron
13. __ Squadron – RAF squadron shot down over the Channel, killing Blanche Breen's young man
14. ZA___ – rocket ship flown to the T-Mat moonbase by the Doctor
15. Cargo ship C___ – ship whose crew think they are under attack from a Draconian battle cruiser

Acronyms

1. According to Vicki, TARDIS stands for what?
2. While the Third Doctor is its scientific adviser, UNIT stands for what?
3. When the Tenth Doctor comes into contact with it, UNIT stands for what?
4. The full name of Elton Pope's society LINDA is what?
5. On Gallifrey, CIA stands for what?

6. According to Susan, TARDIS stands for what?
7. The full name of the Library's CAL is what?
8. IMC, as encountered by the Doctor and Jo on Uxarieus, stands for what?
9. SRS, as headed by Miss Winters, stands for what?
10. Professor Yana's name has a double meaning – what does YANA stand for?

*

11. According to Jackson Lake, TARDIS stands for what?
12. TOMTIT, as created by the Master, stands for what?
13. Mnemonic: what phrase is used by Clara to remember the Maitlands' wi-fi password, RYCBAR123?
14. What does BOSS – Global Chemicals' computer – stand for?
15. What does FOTO – an organisation of which the Doctor and Donna are accused of being members – stand for?

I Think I'd Rather Have a Pint

1. What is the name of the pub in Devil's End?
2. What is the name of the inn where Victorian Clara works?
3. What is the name of the innkeeper who sat out three bouts of plague in her inn?
4. Which drinking establishment visited by the First Doctor has a ballad written about it?
5. What hotel and bar is run by Pat and Elizabeth Rowlinson?

6. Which companion says he wants to 'sit in a pub and drink a pint of beer again'?
7. What inn is frequented by Jules Renan and Jean?
8. What is the name of the pub in Devesham?
9. What is the name of the Cornish innkeeper who is murdered by Cherub?
10. What is the name of the inn on the Calais road where Napoleon meets Barrass?

*

11. What is the name of the inn where Polly and Kirsty pose as orange sellers?
12. What Perivale hotel bar does Ace visit in search of her friends?
13. What is the name of the inn run by a seventh son of a seventh son?
14. Sarah and Stuart are expecting people from what pub to come to their wedding?
15. Which pub football team does Craig's mate Sean think they'll annihilate next week with the Doctor on their side?

Closing Credits (2)

Initially – J

1. What J's form is adopted by Mother of Mine?
2. What J are rhino-like galactic law enforcement officers?
3. What J is a rebel on Varos?
4. What J is the rarest and most valuable element in the galaxy, according to the Graff Vynda-K?
5. What J is the owner of the Palace Theatre where Li H'Sen Chang performs?

6. What J is a direct descendant of the tropical rainforest?
7. What J is the real name of the Empty Child?
8. What J is Miss Winters's assistant at the SRS?
9. What J is a teetotal member of Striker's crew?
10. What J is loved and killed by Tasembeker?

11. What J is a member of the Cult of Skaro?
12. What J is the planet of which Azmael was once the master?
13. What J is one of the Sisters of Plentitude, the first to die when the plague carriers are released?
14. What J is the leader of the Elders who absorbed the First Doctor's energy?
15. What J is the professor who discovered a cure for Spectrox Toxaemia?

Initially – K

1. What K are the ancestors of the Daleks?
2. What K can be 'of Rassilon' or 'to Time'?
3. What K can only be seen by Vincent van Gogh?
4. What K are crystalline creatures who enslave the Gonds?
5. What K is the Great Architect?

6. What K is a diamond belonging to Queen Victoria?
7. What K becomes a hero of Deffry Vale High School?
8. What K is home to Eldrad?
9. What K is a character from the Hourly Telepress?
10. What K is Nyssa's stepmother?

11. What K swallows a holy relic and becomes gigantic?
12. What K is the constellation where Gallifrey is found?
13. What K is an aborigine who was kidnapped by Monarch?
14. What K is the planet that hosts the Daleks' Galactic Council meeting?
15. What K is the planet that Peri allegedly becomes queen of?

Initially – L

1. What L is a professor who creates a Genetic Manipulation Device?
2. What L is the village where Amy and Rory grow up?
3. What L is the planet of mathematicians who use Block Transfer Computation?
4. What L is Sarah Jane's aunt?
5. What L is home to Global Chemicals and the Nuthutch?

6. What L is a stagehand who gets turned into a pig slave?
7. What L is John, who becomes the Cyber Controller?
8. What L is Tim, psychic schoolboy taught by John Smith?
9. What L is the Brotherhood to which Kaftan and Klieg belong?
10. What L is the part of the body of a Birastrop that has a methane filter?

*

11. What L is the university where River Song gains her doctorate?
12. What L is the theatre where Tallulah performs?
13. What L is the planet on which the dish Gaffabeque originates?
14. What L is the city to which the Nobles are evacuated in an alternative timeline?
15. What L drowns on dry land in the sixteenth century?

Opening Titles (3)

Initially – M

1. What M is a snake-headed woman from the Land of Fiction?
2. What M is Wilf's surname?
3. What M is the repository of all knowledge on Gallifrey?
4. What M is the large creature used by the Silurians to aid their attack on Sea Base Four?
5. What M is Richard, once a noted thespian of the seventeenth century?

6. What M is the plant that Werewolves either are, or think they are, allergic to?
7. What M is a computer built by Drax?
8. What M is the name Van Statten gives to the Dalek in his possession?
9. What M is the childhood friend that Amy paradoxically names her daughter after?
10. What M owns a television shop in 1950s London?

*

11. What M is a mobile black eye with a hypnotic stare?
12. What M is the boyband that supports Mr Saxon?
13. What M is the country where Donna and Lance were going on honeymoon?
14. What M is the Detective Inspector who is pursuing Lady Christina?
15. What M is the race of which Chantho is the last survivor?

Initially – N

1. What N is the president who helps the Doctor fight the Silence?
2. What N is the companion that the Doctor first meets on Traken?
3. What N is Joshua, who wants to give his daughter immortality?
4. What N is a bull-headed monster who demands sacrifice from Skonnos?
5. What N is Davros's right-hand man during the creation of the Daleks?

6. What N is the beacon that later becomes the Ark in Space?
7. What N is a Neanderthal preserved by Light?
8. What N is the surname of Sally Sparrow's friend Kathy?
9. What N is the Empty Child's mummy?
10. What N does Donna think they might find Enid Blyton having tea with?

*

11. What N is the prawnlike part of the Swarm that uses the Doctor as a host?
12. What N is the emperor who was told by the Doctor that 'an army marches on its stomach'?
13. What N is the power complex used by the Axons?
14. What N is the city where John Smith's father was a watchmaker?
15. What N is the strong metal that forms a makeshift bridge on the *Titanic*?

Initially – O

1. What O is the Time Lord hero who ends up in a universe of antimatter?
2. What O is the US president who, like almost everyone else on Earth, turns into the Master?
3. What O is a planet neighbouring the Sense-Sphere?
4. What O is Victorian Clara's middle name?
5. What O are the ape-like servants of the Daleks?

6. What O is the home planet of the Kraals?
7. What O is an astrologer who the Doctor met in the Pit?
8. What O is the bird that had a wingspan of fifty feet and blew fire through its nostrils, according to Cassandra?
9. What O is the race that includes Sutekh and Horus?
10. What O is the computer that is keeper of the Minyan race banks?

11. What O is the name for the humans who govern Solos?
12. What O are the stone servants of Cessair of Diplos?
13. What O allows Captain Jack to call anything with a speaker grille?
14. What O is Martha's cousin Adeola's surname?
15. What O do the Tribe of Gum hope will bring them fire?

Episode Three
Behind the Scenes

The Producers

Identify the following producers from their initials:

1. RTD
2. SM
3. JNT
4. VL
5. PH

6. GW
7. BL
8. JW
9. PC
10. IL

11. SL
12. TS
13. DS
14. MW
15. PVW

The Directors 1

Identify the following directors from their initials:

1. DC
2. EL
3. MEB
4. WS
5. JA

6. DZ
7. TDVC
8. TH
9. LB
10. PJ

11. NH
12. FB
13. MI
14. MOM
15. BG

The Directors 2

Identify the following directors from their initials:

1. GH
2. AT
3. CC
4. HM
5. KB

6. GS
7. JG
8. GSF
9. HD
10. PB

11. DB
12. SW
13. GM
14. HH
15. MLS

The Script Editors

Identify the following script/story editors from their initials:

1. TD
2. RH
3. DA
4. CHB
5. ES

6. DW
7. DT
8. AC
9. HR
10. GR

11. VP
12. GD
13. ER
14. LA
15. NS

The Composers

Identify the following composers from their initials:

1. TC
2. RRB
3. MC
4. MG
5. MA

6. DG
7. RL
8. PH
9. GB
10. CB

11. NK
12. RH
13. LP
14. DH
15. HS

The Writers

Identify the following writers from their initials:

1. TN
2. PC
3. BH
4. MH
5. GR

6. KP
7. BA
8. ISB
9. RBS
10. TW

11. NC
12. MK
13. WE
14. PRN
15. BC

One-Hit Wonders

Some writers have written only a single *Doctor Who* television story (as of 2013). Which story was written by:

1. Richard Curtis?
2. Rona Munro?
3. James Moran?
4. Robert Shearman?
5. Anthony Coburn?

6. Peter Ling?
7. Victor Pemberton?
8. Marc Platt?
9. Glen McCoy?
10. Simon Nye?

11. Keith Temple?
12. Matthew Jacobs?
13. Kevin Clarke?
14. Geoffrey Orme?
15. Anthony Steven?

Bubbling Lumps of Hate

Just what was inside a Dalek casing? Well, usually one of these men. Identify the credited Dalek operators from their initials:

1. JSM
2. BE
3. NP
4. CT
5. KM

6. GT
7. DH
8. AS
9. TS
10. KA

11. DB
12. KT
13. TB
14. MS
15. SC

Working Titles 1

Which *Doctor Who* stories were known by the following names at some stage in their production:

1. 'The Zarbi'?
2. 'The Dream Lord'?
3. 'Cubed'?
4. 'Cat-Flap'?
5. 'The Monk'?

6. 'River's Run'?
7. 'The Year of the Moon'?
8. 'Wounded Time'?
9. 'Theatre of Doom'?
10. 'Strange Matter'?

11. 'The Rocks of Doom'?
12. 'Invasion of the Plague Men'?
13. 'Moon of Death'?
14. 'The Mo-Hole Project'?
15. 'What Are Little Boys Made of'?

Working Titles 2

Which *Doctor Who* stories were known by the following names at some stage in their production:

1. 'The Day God Went Mad'?
2. 'The Argolins'?
3. 'Torchwood Falls'?
4. 'His Darkest Hour'?
5. 'The Cyberman Planet'?

6. 'Genesis of Terror'?
7. 'The Last Cyberman'?
8. 'Parallel World'?
9. 'Die Hard in Downing Street'?
10. 'The Angels Wept'?

11. 'The Golden Star'?
12. 'Phantoms of the Hex'?
13. 'Return of the Daleks'?
14. 'Doom of Destiny'?
15. Peepshow?

Working Titles 3

Match the episodes to the individual episode titles they had at some stage in their production:

1. 'Return to Varga'   *An Unearthly Child* 4 ('The Firemaker')

2. 'Is There a Doctor in the Horse'?   *The Daleks* 6 ('The Ordeal')

3. 'Land of the Pharaohs'   *The Daleks* 7 ('The Rescue')

4. 'The Four Dimensions of Time'   *Planet of Giants* 2 ('Dangerous Journey')

5. 'Centre of Terror'   *The Web Planet* 6 ('The Centre')

6. 'The Caves of Terror'   *The Crusade* 2 ('The Knight of Jaffa')

7. 'The Paradox'   *The Crusade* 3 ('The Wheel of Fortune')

8. 'Damsel in Distress'   *The Space Museum* 1 ('The Space Museum')

9. 'The Dawn of Knowledge'   *The Space Museum* 4 ('The Final Phase')

10. 'The Mutation of Time'   *The Time Meddler* 1 ('The Watcher')

11. 'Death in the Afternoon' *The Myth Makers* 3 ('Death of a Spy')

12. 'Zone Seven' *The Daleks' Master Plan* 5 ('Counter Plot')

13. 'The Execution' *The Daleks' Master Plan* 9 ('Golden Death')

14. 'Changing Fortunes' *The Daleks' Master Plan* 10 ('Escape Switch')

15. 'There's Something Just Behind You' *The Daleks' Master Plan* 12 ('The Destruction of Time')

By Any Other Name

NB More than one question may have the same answer!

1. Which companion was at one stage going to be called Lola McGovern?
2. Which companion was at one stage going to be called Cliff?
3. Which companion was at one stage going to be called Michael?
4. Which companion was at one stage going to be called Bridget (Biddy for short)?
5. Which companion was at one stage going to be called Tanni?

6. Which companion was at one stage going to be called Bruck?
7. Which companion was at one stage going to be called Alf?
8. Which companion was at one stage going to be called Lukki?
9. Which companion was at one stage going to be called Sue?
10. Which companion was at one stage going to be called Millie?

*

11. Which companion was at one stage going to be called Richard (Rich for short)?
12. Which companion was at one stage going to be called Valerie?
13. Which companion was at one stage going to be replaced by a companion called Nik?
14. Due to some confusion, which companion ended up with one of her prospective first names as her surname?
15. Which companion was at one stage going to be replaced by a companion called Saida?

Haven't I Seen You Somewhere Before? 1

Many faces pop up in *Doctor Who* more than once. Who played:

1. A Doctor and a Gallifreyan commander?
2. A Doctor and a Pompeian marble trader?
3. A soothsayer and a kissogram?
4. A priestess and a history teacher?
5. A trainee doctor and her cousin?

6. A Yeti and a UNIT sergeant?
7. An American tourist and a space pilot?
8. A sailor and a naval officer?
9. A revered engineer and a Daemon?
10. A revered engineer and a creator of TOMTIT?

11. An expectorating solicitor and a spiky cyborg?
12. A naval captain and a giant slug?
13. A murderer from Marinus and a sorceress?
14. An army lieutenant and a UNIT colonel?
15. A pilot and a scheming count?

Haven't I Seen You Somewhere Before? 2

Some faces have not only popped up in Doctor Who more than once, they've appeared on both sides of the pre- and post-2005 divide. Who played:

1. A nurse and a blood-drinking hospital patient?
2. The Typhonian Beast and the voice of the Beast?
3. A king and a professor?
4. A nearly companion and a queen?
5. An Eternal captain and a shopworker?

6. A plague victim and a spaceship captain?
7. A gas company director and a faceless grandma?
8. A theatre owner and a colonel?
9. An embalmer and a historian?
10. A Solonian and an undertaker?

11. A security officer and a Cyber collaborator?
12. A Mentor servant and a companion's dad?
13. A werewolf and the voice of a monarch?
14. A TV viewer and a companion's gran?
15. A nurse (uncredited) and a neighbour of the Tylers?

Odd One Out 1

These actors appeared in many episodes of *Doctor Who* – but which one of these stories did they *not* feature in?

1. Peter Miles: *The Dominators; Doctor Who and the Silurians; Invasion of the Dinosaurs; Genesis of the Daleks*
2. Philip Madoc: *The Krotons; The War Games; Carnival of Monsters; The Power of Kroll*
3. John Ringham: *The Aztecs; The Smugglers; The Ice Warriors; Colony in Space*
4. Jimmy Vee: *The End of the World; Aliens of London; Tooth and Claw; Voyage of the Damned*
5. Michael Sheard: *Planet of Giants; The Ark; The Mind of Evil; Castrovalva*

6. John Woodnutt: *The Wheel in Space; Spearhead from Space; Frontier in Space; Terror of the Zygons*
7. Laurence Payne: *The Gunfighters; The Leisure Hive; Terminus; The Two Doctors*
8. Michael Kilgariff: *The Tomb of the Cybermen; Frontier in Space; Revenge of the Cybermen; Attack of the Cybermen*
9. Kevin Lindsay: *The Time Warrior; Planet of the Spiders; The Ark in Space; The Sontaran Experiment*

10. George Pravda: *The Enemy of the World*; *The Mutants*; *The Deadly Assassin*; *Nightmare of Eden*

11. Christopher Tranchell: *The Massacre*; *The Smugglers*; *The Faceless Ones*; *The Invasion of Time*

12. Hugh Walters: *The Chase*; *The Web of Fear*; *The Deadly Assassin*; *Revelation of the Daleks*

13. John Bailey: *The Sensorites*; *The Evil of the Daleks*; *The Masque of Mandragora*; *The Horns of Nimon*

14. Barry Jackson: *The Romans*; *Galaxy 4*; *The Gunfighters*; *The Armageddon Factor*

15. Clare Jenkins: *The Savages*; *The Macra Terror*; *The Wheel in Space*; *The War Games*

Odd One Out 2

These actors appeared in many episodes of *Doctor Who* – but which one of these stories did they *not* feature in?

1. James Bree: *The War Games*; *Colony in Space*; *Full Circle*; *The Ultimate Foe*
2. Sonny Caldinez: *The Evil of the Daleks*; *The Tomb of the Cybermen*; *The Ice Warriors*; *The Seeds of Death*
3. David Collings: *Revenge of the Cybermen*; *The Robots of Death*; *Mawdryn Undead*; *The Twin Dilemma*
4. Bernard Horsfall: *The Mind Robber*; *The War Games*; *Planet of the Daleks*; *Genesis of the Daleks*
5. Martin Jarvis: *The Web Planet*; *Invasion of the Dinosaurs*; *The Stones of Blood*; *Vengeance on Varos*

6. Frederick Jaeger: *The Savages*; *Planet of Evil*; *The Invisible Enemy*; *Arc of Infinity*
7. Tony Caunter: *The Crusade*; *Colony in Space*; *Planet of Evil*; *Enlightenment*
8. Sheila Dunn: *The Daleks' Master Plan*; *The Invasion*; *Inferno*; *Terror of the Zygons*
9. Peter Halliday: *The Invasion*; *The Face of Evil*; *City of Death*; *Remembrance of the Daleks*

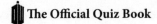

10. Donald Pickering: *The Keys of Marinus; The Faceless Ones; Underworld; Time and the Rani*

11. Christopher Burgess: *The Enemy of the World; The Invasion; Terror of the Autons; Planet of the Spiders*

12. Norman Jones: *The Abominable Snowmen; Doctor Who and the Silurians; Robot; The Masque of Mandragora*

13. Paul Kasey: *Love & Monsters; Turn Left; Planet of the Dead; The Doctor, the Widow and the Wardrobe*

14. Rex Robinson: *The Three Doctors; The Monster of Peladon; The Hand of Fear; Logopolis*

15. Ivor Salter: *The Space Museum; The Myth Makers; The Deadly Assassin; Black Orchid*

Name Share

Complete the following to give the names of two actors who have appeared in *Doctor Who*. The role (or one of the roles) they played in is given in brackets.

1. (Liz) Caroline _____ Hurt (The War Doctor)
2. (Ian) William _____ Tovey (Midshipman Frame)
3. (Adam Colby) Edward _____ Darvill (Rory)
4. (Areta) Geraldine _____ Armstrong (Arwell)
5. (Kerensky) David _____ Crowden (Soldeed)

6. (Dibber) Glen _____ Grumbar (Dalek)
7. (Anat) Anna _____ Jackson (Drax)
8. (Tilda) Brenda _____ Purchase (Pirate Captain)
9. (Nyder) Peter _____ Fothergill (SV7)
10. (Farel) Stephen ____ Woolgar (Staff Sergeant Arnold)

11. (Vural) Donald _____ Sheldon (Kirksen)
12. (Eldred) Philip ___ Barrett (Bennett)
13. (Priam) Max _____ Gibbs (The Watcher)
14. (Aukon) Emrys _____ Maxwell (Jackson)
15. (The Destroyer) Marek _____ Diffling (De Flores)

Location, Location, Location 1 – Home

It's not just quarries! Filming for which story took place in or near:

1. Madame Tussaud's?
2. Gatwick Airport?
3. Heathrow Airport?
4. Robert Brothers' Circus?
5. No-Man's Land Fort in the Solent?

6. Leeds Castle?
7. Dover Castle?
8. The Royal Albert Hall?
9. Singleton Hospital?
10. Middlesex Polytechnic?

11. Bodiam Castle?
12. Arundel Castle?
13. Peckforton Castle?
14. Stradey Castle?
15. Milford Chest Hospital?

Location, Location, Location 2 – Away

The vast majority of *Doctor Who* is filmed in the UK, but occasionally production teams have ventured further afield.

Location filming for which story or stories took place in:

1. Rome, Italy?
2. Amsterdam, Netherlands?
3. Paris, France?
4. New York (Tenth Doctor)?
5. New York (Eleventh Doctor)?

6. Lanzarote, Spain?
7. Seville, Spain?
8. Vancouver, Canada?
9. Utah, USA?
10. Dubai, UAE?

*

11. Almeira, Spain?
12. Trogir, Croatia (1)?
13. Trogir, Croatia (2)?
14. Which country was to provide the location for the unmade Sixth Doctor story 'Yellow Fever and How to Cure It'?
15. Back to the UK: what was the first story to feature Welsh location filming?

Surprise, Surprise

Anagrams have been used in *Doctor Who* for inspiration, to hide a story element or to fool onlookers…

1. What monster's name is an anagram of Gourmand?
2. What monster's name is an anagram of Dishrag?
3. What race's name is an anagram of the creations they would later become?
4. What anagram was used by the 2005 production office to label *Doctor Who* preview prints?
5. What substance is an anagram of Holy Grail?

6. What character's name is an anagram of (famous mathematician) Dirac?
7. What monster's name is an anagram of Attractor?
8. What monster's name is an anagram of 'Star Pet'?
9. What device is an anagram of Earth's Gone?
10. What anagram featured in the credits of *Remembrance of the Daleks* to disguise Davros's presence?

*

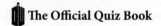

11. What anagram was used in the credits of *Time-Flight* to disguise the Master's presence?

12. What anagram was used in the credits of *Castrovalva* to disguise the Master's presence?

13. What anagram was used in the credits of *The King's Demons* to disguise the Master's presence?

14. What anagram was used in the audition process for Amy?

15. What anagram was used in the audition process for Clara?

Guards, Guards

Pity the poor actor who gets a speaking role but isn't even given a name. Match up the actor to the story in which they played a part called simply 'Guard'.

1. *Utopia*   Peter Ducrow
2. *The Hand of Fear*   Harry Fielder
3. *The Sun Makers*   Joe Jacobs
4. *The Pandorica Opens*   Robert Luckham
5. *The Five Doctors*   Richard Steele

6. *Fury from the Deep*   John Caesar
7. *Terror of the Vervoids*   John Tallents
8. *The Mark of the Rani*   Tim Goodman
9. *The Time Monster*   Alan James
10. *The Keys of Marinus*   Hugh Beverton

11. *The Power of the Daleks*   Robert Forknall
12. *The Macra Terror*   Tom Kelly
13. *The Seeds of Doom*   Melville Jones
14. *The Pirate Planet*   Robin Hargrave
15. *The Savages*   Adam Kurakin

Missing Episodes

All questions refer to the situation as of April 2014, with 97 episodes of *Doctor Who* still missing from the archives. The discovery of an episode or story is here dated to the year when the discovery was announced.

1. Who was the photographer who produced the Telesnaps?
2. There are three stories which have no surviving footage at all. *Marco Polo* and *The Massacre* are two; what is the third?
3. Which producer of black-and-white *Doctor Who* had no Telesnaps taken during his time on the programme?
4. In which country was *The Tomb of the Cybermen* discovered in 1991?
5. Which was the only episode of *The Web of Fear* not returned to the archives in 2013?

6. Four Patrick Troughton stories are completely missing (although all have some footage in existence). *The Power of the Daleks*, *The Highlanders* and *Fury from the Deep* are three; what is the fourth?
7. Which companion (or companions) features in more missing episodes than any other companion?
8. Which companions have the greatest proportion of their

    episodes missing?

9.   What was the last story for which Telesnaps are known to have been taken?

10. Which actor took screenshots of the broadcast of 'The Feast of Steven', the only surviving visuals from that episode?

11. Two episodes of which story were discovered in the basement of a Mormon church (previously a BBC property)?

12. Three actors played the character Malpha in *Mission to the Unknown* and *The Daleks' Master Plan*. Which is the only one of whom there are no surviving in-character images?

13. In what year did the official 'junkings' stop?

14. What is the only missing episode for which Telesnaps are known to have been taken but which no longer exist?

15. What is believed to be the first story to have had its transmission mastertapes junked?

Do You Remember the First Time?

What was the first *Doctor Who* story:

1. To be broadcast in colour?
2. To credit the lead character as 'the Doctor'?
3. To be produced in 3D (charity specials aside)?
4. To feature location filming?
5. To be shot entirely on film?

6. To be released on home video?
7. To feature the Doctor's face in the opening titles?
8. To use Colour Separation Overlay?
9. To feature subtitles?
10. To feature the 1970s 'diamond logo'?

11. To use stunt team HAVOC?
12. To have location filming at a quarry?
13. To shoot both locations and studio entirely on videotape?
14. To be recorded in High Definition?
15. To have an on-screen copyright date?

The Other Side of the Camera

In which story can you find:

1. Writer Mark Gatiss as a monstrous professor?
2. Writer Glyn Jones as a colonist?
3. Producer John Nathan-Turner shooing away some passers-by?
4. Producer Derrick Sherwin as a UNIT commissionaire?
5. Producer Marcus Wilson's photo on a wall?

6. Director Douglas Camfield driving a car?
7. Composer Murray Gold as a musician?
8. Writer Robert Banks Stewart as a Time Lord?
9. Writer Victor Pemberton as a scientist?
10. Composer Dudley Simpson as a conductor?

11. Director Andrew Morgan as a tourist?
12. Director Timothy Combe in a gun battle?
13. Director Michael E. Briant as a radio DJ?
14. Producer Barry Letts voicing monsters?
15. Assistant script editor Trevor Ray as a ticket collector?

Costume Capers 1

1. Which story features olive-drab Daleks?
2. Which story features a wooden Cyberman?
3. Which story features Sea Devils in armour?
4. Which post-2005 story features Cybermen with rounded faces?
5. Which was the first story to feature two-eyed Silurians?

6. Which story features a Cybermat with sharp teeth?
7. Which story features a tall Sontaran with a beard?
8. Which story features the White Guardian wearing a straw hat and a carnation?
9. Which story features the Black Guardian with a white beard and wearing a white coif?
10. Which is the first story to feature white Daleks with gold 'skirt bumps'?

*

11. Which story (briefly) features a Dalek with alternate base panels on its 'skirt' painted black?
12. Which is the first story to feature a gold Dalek?
13. Which was the first story to feature Cybermen with 'teardrop' eyes?
14. Which story features a Dalek with red flashing dome lights?
15. Which story features a Dalek with a steel syringe instead of a plunger?

Costume Capers 2

1. Which story features 'stone' Daleks?
2. Which story features a glass Dalek?
3. Which story features 'stocking-faced' Cybermen?
4. Which story features large, eyeless Cybermats?
5. Which story features Sea Devils with 'fishing net' tunics?

6. Which story features an all-black Cyberman?
7. Which story features Cybermats with antennae?
8. Which is the first story to feature Sontarans in blue armour?
9. Which is the first story to feature the Black Guardian with a bird in his hair?
10. Which story features the White Guardian with a bird in his hair?

*

11. Which story features Sontarans with five fingers on each hand?
12. Which story features Daleks with discs on their backs?
13. Which story features a movie Dalek in gold with black 'skirt' panels and gold 'skirt bumps'?
14. Which is the first story to feature silver Daleks with black domes?
15. Which was the first story to feature Daleks with 'solar slats' at their 'shoulders'?

Dressing for the Occasion

1. Who designed the Daleks?
2. Which monsters were given baseball mitts for hands in a redesign?
3. Who created the Fourth Doctor's original look?
4. Which monsters had heads made from fox-terrier skulls?
5. Which company built props including the original Daleks and the Macra?

6. Who created the Seventh Doctor's look?
7. Who built the first Dalek prop for the 2005 revival?
8. What company made the redesigned Ice Warrior for *Cold War*?
9. Who designed the Fourth Doctor's 'burgundy' costume for his final season?
10. Who created the original Davros mask?

*

11. Which monsters had yak hair on their heads and ping-pong balls for eyes?
12. Who created the Sixth Doctor's look?
13. Who created the Third Doctor's look?
14. Which monsters had heads formed from plastic weasel skulls?
15. Who created the Twelfth Doctor's look?

Credit Crunch

1. Which is the only story to feature the credit 'Doctor Who Peter Davison'?
2. Which story features the credit 'The BBC wish to acknowledge the help given to them by the Royal Navy in the making of this programme'?
3. Which story features a credit for 'Insect Movement'?
4. What was the last story to credit Jenna Coleman as 'Jenna-Louise Coleman'?
5. Which story is known simply as 'Invasion' in the opening titles of its first episode?

6. Which story features the credit 'The BBC wish to acknowledge the help given to them by the Ministry of Defence in the making of this programme'?
7. An episode of which story features a credit for 'Yate's Guard' (sic)?
8. What is John Hurt credited as for *The Day of the Doctor*?
9. Which story features a credit for Murphy 'Grunbar' rather than Murphy Grumbar?
10. Which story features the dedication 'In memory of Verity Lambert OBE 1935–2007'?

11. What actor's first name is misspelt in the (broadcast) credits to episodes one and two of *Ghost Light*?
12. Which story features a credit for 'Hero Pig'?
13. Which story features a credit for 'Kitt' Pedler rather than Kit Pedler?
14. Which is the only Fourth Doctor story to call its episodes 'Episodes' rather than 'Parts'?
15. An episode of which story features a credit for 'Derek' Sherwin rather than Derrick Sherwin?

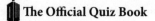

The Men Inside the Monsters

Many men have played many monsters - but which actor played each exact combination of roles? (NB Every monster type they played is not necessarily listed.) Who played:

1. Giant Robot / Ogron / Cyberman?
2. Daemon / Ogron / Kastrian?
3. Silurian / Planetarian / Sea Devil / Primitive?
4. Mentor / Sontaran?
5. Wooden monarch / Ice Warrior / Minotaur?

6. Ood / Slitheen / Zygon / Tritovore?
7. Kraal / Sontaran / Wirrn?
8. Fungoid / Mechonoid / Mire Beast / Planetarian?
9. Ood / Cybershade / Tritovore / Scarecrow?
10. Slyther / Dalek?

11. Macra / Zarbi / Dalek?
12. Aridian / Optera?
13. Monoid / White Robot / Cyberman?
14. Cyberman / Zygon / Crooked Man?
15. Cyberman / Yeti / Ice Warrior?

The Voice

Some characters' or creatures' dialogue has been provided by voice artists. (NB The actors may have played other roles in *Doctor Who*, but these were their only voice-only performances.) Who or what was given voice by:

1. David Brierley?
2. Struan Rodger?
3. Zoe Wanamaker?
4. Sir Ian McKellen?
5. John Dearth?

6. Maureen Morris?
7. Robert Cartland?
8. Gerald Taylor?
9. David de Keyser?
10. Catherine Fleming?

11. Heron Carvic?
12. Noah Johnson?
13. Christine Pollon?
14. Terry Bale?
15. Martin Gower?

Ratings War

1. Which Doctor has the highest viewing figures for his final episode?
2. Which Doctor has the highest viewing figures for his first full episode?
3. What was the first episode from 2005 onwards to have viewing figures over 10 million?
4. Which episode is not only the highest-rated *Doctor Who* Christmas special but also has the highest viewing figures for any episode from 2005 onwards?
5. *Destiny of the Daleks* and *City of Death* have the top two highest viewing figures for all of *Doctor Who* – why are their figures so high?

6. Which episode has the highest viewing figures for all of *Doctor Who*?
7. Which story has the lowest average viewing figures for all of *Doctor Who*?
8. Put these multiple-Doctor stories in order of average viewing figures, from highest to lowest: *The Three Doctors, The Five Doctors, The Two Doctors, The Day of the Doctor.*
9. Which Christmas special from 2005 onwards has the lowest viewing figures?

10. What was the first *Doctor Who* episode to be in the BBC's weekly Top Ten most-watched programmes?

11. Which was the first episode from 2005 onwards to fall outside the Top 20?

12. What was the first story to have over 10 million viewers for each of its episodes?

13. Apart from the first ever episode, which was the first episode to fall outside the BBC's weekly Top 100 most-watched programmes?

14. Which was the first episode to get over 10 million viewers?

15. Which was the first episode to be in the BBC's weekly Top Five most-watched programmes?

Titles and Tunes

1. Who composed the *Doctor Who* theme tune?
2. Who created the original arrangement of the theme tune?
3. What shape do the letters 'DW' form in the logo of the Eleventh Doctor's first two seasons?
4. Who arranged the title music for the Ninth, Tenth and Eleventh Doctors' eras?
5. What was the first story to feature the TARDIS in the opening titles?

6. Whose arrangement of the title theme debuted on *The Leisure Hive*?
7. What was the last story to feature the 'neon' logo (a logo designed to look like it's made out of a continuous length of neon tubing) in its titles?
8. Which BBC department was responsible for realising and recording the original theme?
9. What was the only season to use the Dominic Glynn arrangement of the theme tune?
10. Which Doctor actor released a record of the theme tune with spoken verse over the top?

*

11. What was the first story to see the main cast listed in its opening titles?
12. A new theme tune created with the 'Delaware' synthesizer was rejected – but was heard on UK TV in 1972 in a trailer for which story?
13. What story from 2005 onwards was the first to feature the Doctor's face in the opening titles?
14. What was the first story to feature a musical 'sting' leading into the closing theme?
15. Who arranged the theme tune for the 1996 TV movie?

Gossip Column

Spouses or relatives of Doctors, companions or series regulars have sometimes joined the show themselves. Identify the actor and their role in *Doctor Who*. (NB marriages and roles are not necessarily concurrent.)

1. The Tenth Doctor's wife – and daughter
2. The Fourth Doctor's wife – and companion
3. Victoria's Yeti-hunting father
4. Romana's husband, the television commentator
5. Polly's husband, the terrifying toymaker.

6. The Third Doctor's wife – and the First Doctor's companion
7. The Sixth Doctor's wife, a space pirate
8. The Master's wife, with eight legs
9. The Second Doctor's son, who proposed to the Third Doctor's companion
10. The Master's wife – and the Third Doctor's companion

*

11. Liz Shaw's niece, a mathematical child
12. The Tenth Doctor's father, in service
13. Turlough's colourful wife
14. The Rani's husband, a captain-turned-plant
15. The Rani's husband, a companion's brother

Soap Suds 1

1. Which *Doctor Who* actor went on to play *Emmerdale Farm*'s Joe Sugden?
2. Which *Doctor Who* actor was once *Neighbours*' Charlene Mitchell?
3. Which *Doctor Who* actor went on to play *Brookside*'s Penny Crosbie?
4. Which *Doctor Who* actor was once *Emmerdale*'s Jasmine Thomas?
5. Which *Doctor Who* actor went on to play *EastEnders*' Rosa di Marco?

6. Which *Doctor Who* director went on to co-create *EastEnders*?
7. Which *Doctor Who* producer went on to produce *Coronation Street*?
8. Charity special *Dimensions in Time* was a crossover with which soap opera?
9. Which *Doctor Who* actor went on to play *Coronation Street*'s Ted Sullivan?
10. Which *Doctor Who* actor went on to play *Casualty*'s Elizabeth Straker?

*

11. Script editor Derrick Sherwin and his successor Terrance Dicks had both written previously for which soap?
12. Which religion-based soap opera was created by Russell T Davies?
13. Which *Doctor Who* actor went on to play *Emmerdale Farm*'s Denis Rigg?
14. Which *Doctor Who* writer co-created 1960s soap opera *Compact*?
15. Which supernatural soap included Russell T Davies, Gareth Roberts and Paul Cornell among its crew?

Soap Suds 2

In which *Doctor Who* story or stories can you find:

1. *EastEnders'* Dirty Den as a mercenary?
2. *Coronation Street's* Gail as a young colonist?
3. *EastEnders'* Dot as a lady of the Middle Ages?
4. *Prisoner: Cell Block H's* Andrew Reynolds as a Thal leader?
5. *The Archers'* Mike Tucker as the creator of the Daleks?

6. *The Bill's* Reg Hollis appearing in a dream?
7. *Waterloo Road's* Chalky as a fan of the Doctor?
8. *EastEnders'* Tanya Manning as a game-show contestant?
9. *Hollyoaks'* Liz Burton Taylor as an innkeeper?
10. *EastEnders'* Dr Oliver as a paediatrician?

11. *Prisoner: Cell Block H's* Zara Moonbeam as a spaceship crewmember?
12. *The Archers'* Nelson Gabriel as a space general?
13. *Crossroads'* Shughie McFee as a pub landlord?
14. *Family Affairs'* Angus Hart as a warrior?
15. *Pobol Y Cym's* Sergeant James as a London policeman?

Stage Names and Pseudonyns

1. By what name is (Doctor) Mr Moffett better known?
2. By what name is (companion) Mr Enoch better known?
3. By what name is (companion) Lady Sarah better known?
4. By what name is (Doctor) Mr McDonald better known?
5. *The Brain of Morbius* is credited to Robin Bland – but who really wrote it?

6. By what name is (companion) Lianne better known?
7. By what name is (companion) Thomas better known?
8. By what name is (Doctor) Percy Kent-Smith better known?
9. *The Daemons* is credited to Guy Leopold – but who really wrote it?
10. *The Dominators* is credited to Norman Ashby – but who really wrote it?

*

11. By what name is (companion) Ms Mahoney better known?
12. By what name is (companion) Mr Woods better known?
13. *Pyramids of Mars* is credited to Stephen Harris – but who really wrote it?
14. *The Invasion of Time* is credited to David Agnew – but who really wrote it?
15. *City of Death* is also credited to David Agnew – but who really wrote it?

Closing Credits (3)

Initially – P

1. What P is the estate where the Tylers live?
2. What P is the animal inside the spaceship that crashes into Big Ben?
3. What P is a legendary prison beneath Stonehenge?
4. What P is the vent in the back of a Sontaran's neck?
5. What P is Amy turned into while she is in a doll's house?

6. What P is the ship captained by Kath McDonnell?
7. What P are the aliens that are destroyed when Vesuvius erupts?
8. What P is the wife of Nero who is jealous of Barbara?
9. What P is the Dave who isn't Other Dave in River Song's crew?
10. What P is the colour of the furs worn by the Spiridons?

11. What P is Josh, whose energy is drained by the Axons?
12. What P is the country where the Brigadier is stranded during the Sontaran invasion?
13. What P is the stick with which a Venusian shanghorn should never be trusted?
14. What P is the only inbetween in Paradise Towers?
15. What P is a mighty civilisation from the Scarlet System?

Initially – R

1. What R is the founder of the Time Lords?
2. What R is a source of power found in Cardiff?
3. What R is an instrument played by the Second Doctor?
4. What R are the humans controlled by Daleks during their invasion of Earth?
5. What R are locked in an endless war with the Sontarans?

6. What R keeps the Doctor and Romana one step ahead of the Black Guardian?
7. What R is a friendly plumber on Platform One?
8. What R is the home planet of the Slitheen?
9. What R is Luke, child genius who invented ATMOS?
10. What R is Madame de Pompadour's nickname as a child?

11. What R is a Dalek unit of measurement?
12. What R is Experimental Propotype K1?
13. What R, according to the Drahvins, are things that crawl and murder?
14. What R is where Terileptils are sent to work in the tinclavic mines?
15. What R has seasons called Icetime and Suntime?

Initially – S

1. What S is a politician who looks like the Second Doctor?
2. What S do the Doctor and Donna claim their surname to be when they visit Pompeii?
3. What S is the trader who hijacks the Silurian Ark?
4. What S is a planetoid-dwelling servant of the Black Guardian?
5. What S does baby Alfie prefer to be called?

6. What S guards the state strong room on Ribos?
7. What S is the Muto who helps Sarah Jane on Skaro?
8. What S is the guerrilla who is paradoxically guilty of causing the Dalek conquest he is trying to prevent?
9. What S are the green-skinned natives of Delta Magna?
10. What S is the prison where the Keller Machine is tested?

11. What S did the Monk help the Ancient Britons to build?
12. What S is the sort of medicine practised by the Thal Taron?
13. What S is the paradigm the Krillitanes want solved?
14. What S is the rocket Vorus plans to use to destroy the Cybermen?
15. What S is Glitz's home planet?

Opening Titles (4)

Initially – T

1. What T is the alien-fighting institute founded by Queen Victoria?
2. What T is the deadly form of the last humans?
3. What T are the fly-like aliens the Doctor meets on San Helios?
4. What T is the game played by the Doctor and the Celestial Toymaker?
5. What T is a cruiseliner that crashes into the TARDIS?

6. What T is a missile the Master tries to steal?
7. What T is the anthropologist who twice helps the Doctor against the Yetis?
8. What T are the Rani's four-eyed servants?
9. What T do the Doctor and Romana use to locate segments of the Key to Time?
10. What T is the alien race to which George, son of Alex and Claire, belongs?

*

11. What T are the descendants of the Technicians on the Mordee expedition?
12. What T is essential to the Galactic Federation's war effort?
13. What T is the name used by Vorg and Shockeye for humans?
14. What T is Kaftan's servant, who reseals the Cybermen in their tomb?
15. What T is the weapon Professor Rumford took to New York in case she got mugged?

Initially – U

1. What U are the dead in Victorian Cardiff?
2. What U is a celebrated jewel thief of the 1920s?
3. What U is a top-secret military organisation for which the Doctor works as Scientific Adviser?
4. What U is the legendary place that calls to the last members of the human race?
5. What U is the Schism into which the 8-year-old Master is forced to stare?

6. What U is a chamber below Stonehenge?
7. What U is the decryption machine designed by Dr Judson?
8. What U is the race to which the Collector belongs?
9. What U is a pop group of which Professor Grisenko is a big fan?
10. What U is Garron's fellow conman?

11. What U is the title given to the Sontaran Staal?
12. What U is captain of Speedbird Concorde 192?
13. What U does Timanov want to burn on Sarn?
14. What U is commander of the Sandminer?
15. What U is the area of New New York where Pharmacytown is found?

Initially – V

1. What V is Tegan's aunt?
2. What V is the volcano that erupted and buried Pompeii?
3. What V is Tegan's grandfather's surname?
4. What V is a Lurman showman?
5. What V is the Doctor's Victorian Silurian ally?

6. What V is the UNIT carrier ship taken over by the Master?
7. What V is the biggest killer drug in existence, according to the Fourth Doctor?
8. What V is the legendary planet of Gold?
9. What V is the living metal used to make a statue of Lady Peinforte?
10. What V is the first planet the Second Doctor visits?

11. What V vanishes into the Timelash with an amulet?
12. What V does the Doctor help to invade Gallifrey?
13. What V is a major of the Ninth Sontaran Battle Fleet?
14. What V is a trapper who attacks Barbara on Marinus?
15. What V does the Third Doctor say were 'quite decent chaps'?

Episode Four
Monsters, Villains and Aliens

Assault with a Deadly Weapon

Which monster is destroyed or defeated by the use of:

1. Anti-plastic?
2. Vinegar?
3. Fondant surprise?
4. The Doctor's recorder?
5. Cocktail Polly?

6. Water?
7. Metal virus?
8. The Gravitron?
9. Hexachromite gas?
10. The De-mat gun?

11. X-ray laser?
12. Sulphuric acid?
13. Coronic acid?
14. The Isop-Tope?
15. Vionesium?

Name That Villain

Idenitify these villains from their first names. The Doctor they opposed is given in brackets.

1. Mercy (10th)
2. Mehendri (4th)
3. Tobias (2nd)
4. Theodore (2nd)
5. Harrison (4th)

6. Winifred (11th)
7. Hilda (4th)
8. Henry (9th)
9. Max (4th)
10. Jocelyn (3rd)

11. Walter (11th)
12. Joinson (6th)
13. Samuel (1st)
14. Carlos (4th)
15. Maurice (2nd)

Who Are You?

What race or nationality are the following:

1. Scibus, Tarpok, Eldane?
2. Skaldak, Slaar, Rintan?
3. Nyder, Ronson, Gharman?
4. Doomfinger, Bloodtide, Lilith?
5. Rossiter, Addams?

6. Threst, Vast, Varne?
7. Jatt, Casp, Hame?
8. Ky, Varan, Vorn?
9. Mena, Pangol, Morix?
10. Dyoni, Marat, Vaber?

11. Morelli, Vishinsky, Salamar?
12. Sorvin, Praygat?
13. Idmon, Idas, Naia?
14. Malsan, Rynian, Prondyn?
15. Etnin, Tensa, Kando?

Daleks – The 1960s 1

1. What were the Dalek people originally called?
2. What area of England do the Daleks turn into a gigantic mine area?
3. What is the Black Dalek's man-eating pet?
4. What does Barbara use to blind a Dalek?
5. What kills all the Daleks in Section 3 of the Dalek City?

6. Who describes the Daleks as 'motorised dustbins'?
7. What does Ian compare the acrid smell of the Daleks to?
8. What does the Doctor say the Daleks will have to do before attempting to conquer Earth?
9. According to the Doctor, the Daleks they met on Skaro are how far in the future from the Daleks invading Earth?
10. What two disasters weakened the Earth enough for the Daleks to invade?

*

11. Who is the first person to be shot by a Dalek on screen?
12. Who is the first person to be killed by a Dalek on screen?
13. What does the Doctor say is the Thals' great advantage against the Daleks?
14. How long do the Daleks say it would take them to construct a neutron bomb?
15. What do the Daleks use to track vibrations?

Daleks – The 1960s 2

1. What do the Daleks call the Mechonoids?
2. Who is in charge of the Daleks on Kembel?
3. What new attachment do the Daleks have to carry out Operation Inferno?
4. Who stows away on a Dalek time machine after being left behind by the TARDIS?
5. Who do the Daleks attempt to test the Time Destructor on?

6. What Earth city does Vicki say was destroyed in the Dalek invasion?
7. The Daleks held a council for their allies at the same time as what other conference was being held?
8. Who is the first member of the Daleks' alliance to be exterminated?
9. What do the *Mary Celeste*'s crew think the Daleks are?
10. In Ancient Egypt, who is given one hour to retrieve the Taranium core for the Daleks?

*

11. What do the Daleks use to pull the Doctor-hijacked Dalek pursuit ship to Kembel?
12. What creatures do the Daleks exterminate immediately upon arrival on Mira?
13. According to Marc Cory, how many planets in the Ninth Galactic System have the Daleks gained control over in the last 500 years?
14. What instrument of the Daleks causes the Spar to crash on Desperus?
15. According to Lowery, how long before the events of *Mission to the Unknown* did the Daleks invade Earth?

Daleks – The 1960s 3

1. What phrase(s) do the Vulcan Daleks repeat, convincing the colonists that they are harmless?
2. How does a Victorian Dalek refer to birds?
3. What test do the Daleks set for Jamie?
4. What secret do the Daleks promise Maxtible in return for his cooperation?
5. What game do the humanised Daleks play?

6. How many Daleks were originally in the Vulcan capsule?
7. What does the Doctor say is like blood to Daleks?
8. At the end of *The Power of the Daleks*, what sign is the viewer given that the Vulcan Daleks aren't 'just a heap of old iron now'?
9. What do the Daleks threaten to do if Victoria doesn't eat?
10. Who is the first human to receive the Dalek factor?

*

11. How long has the Dalek capsule spent in a mercury swamp on Vulcan, according to Lesterson?
12. Who is the first person killed by a Dalek on Vulcan?
13. What philosophical question does a Dalek ask after shooting Hensell?
14. How many mirrors are used in the experiments that bring the Daleks to the nineteenth century?
15. What five qualities does the Doctor say are in the positronic brains he implants into the Daleks?

Daleks – The 1970s 1

1. What anthropoids are the Daleks using as security guards in the twenty-second century?
2. Who do the guerrillas believe is responsible for the start of the wars that lead to the Dalek invasion?
3. The guerrillas have stolen the formula for what type of explosive from the Daleks?
4. What does the Doctor use liquid colour spray for on Spiridon?
5. Who sends the TARDIS to Spiridon so the Doctor can pursue the Daleks?

6. Who are in charge of the Daleks at the time of their presence on Spiridon?
7. What do the twenty-second-century Daleks use to establish the Doctor's identity?
8. Why does the Doctor advise the Spiridon Thals not to lift the top off a Dalek?
9. How many Daleks do the Thals initially think are on Spiridon?
10. How many Daleks are really on Spiridon?

*

11. What experiments do the Daleks intend to carry out on the Doctor and Codal?
12. By what means does the Daleks' guidance system function, according to Codal?
13. What do the Daleks plan to release into Spiridon's atmosphere?
14. What previous Dalek serial is namechecked in the dialogue of both *The Evil of the Daleks* and *Day of the Daleks* (not including *The Daleks*)?
15. What do the twenty-second-century Daleks use to divert time-travellers to regional control?

Daleks – The 1970s 2

1. What are the Daleks called have before Davros renames them 'Daleks'?
2. What do the humans mistake the Dalek saucer for as it comes in to land on Exxilon?
3. What does the Doctor use to 'impair the visual circuit' of a Dalek on Skaro in *Destiny of the Daleks*?
4. Why did the Daleks return to find Davros?
5. At what point do the Exxilon Daleks say the truce with the humans will end?

6. On Exxilon, what do the Daleks test their new weapons on?
7. How long has Tyssan been a prisoner of the Daleks?
8. Why is Hamilton unhappy at the idea of cooperating with the Daleks?
9. Where did the Daleks keep their captives before bringing them to Skaro?
10. How much explosive are the 'kamikaze' Daleks carrying to destroy the Movellan ship?

*

11. Who is the first person (in Dalek chronology) to be killed by a Dalek?
12. Why does the Doctor think the Daleks want parrinium?
13. Why do the Daleks really want parrinium?
14. What causes one of the Exxilon Daleks to self-destruct?
15. What do the Daleks plan to do once they have left Exxilon?

Daleks – The 1980s

1. What does the Seventh Doctor say the 'little green (Dalek) blobs' are encased in?
2. Which human mercenary was working for the Supreme Dalek in *Resurrection of the Daleks*?
3. What part of the Dalek does Ace aim for with her anti-tank rocket?
4. How does the Doctor upgrade a baseball bat to become a weapon against Daleks?
5. What 1963 Dalek has no eyestalk and a single huge gun?

6. What does the Tranquil Repose DJ use to kill Daleks?
7. Which Dalek faction is the headmaster of Coal Hill controlled by?
8. What adjective does Ace object to in a Dalek's description of her?
9. How many Daleks does Davros gain control of on the space station?
10. Who destroys the space station full of Daleks?

*

11. How do the space station Daleks plan to get control of Earth?
12. What is to happen to Davros's Daleks after his defeat on Necros?
13. What does the Doctor use to destroy the first Dalek at Totters Yard?
14. How do the Movellans finally defeat the Daleks?
15. What is a terminal pastime, according to the Seventh Doctor?

Daleks – 2005 onwards 1

1. Whose DNA does Van Statten's Dalek feed off to regenerate?
2. Who is the leader of the Cult of Skaro?
3. What happens to Dalek prisoners of low intelligence in Manhattan?
4. How did the Cult of Skaro get to 1930?
5. Who accidentally activates the Genesis Ark?

6. How long did it take for the entire Dalek race to be wiped out in the Time War, according to the Ninth Doctor?
7. Which of Van Statten's employees is 'suckered to death'?
8. What protects Gwen and Ianto from the Dalek that is trying to get into the Torchwood hub?
9. What is Van Statten's name for the place he keeps the Dalek?
10. For what purpose was the Cult of Skaro created?

*

11. Which Dalek objects to the Final Experiment, believing Daleks should remain pure?

12. What sort of radiation is needed to splice the Dalek and human genetic codes and awaken the Dalek-humans?

13. Who is the only survivor of the Cult of Skaro at the end of *Evolution of the Daleks*?

14. What did the Master witness the Dalek Emperor taking control of during the Time War?

15. Who destroys the Dalek that exterminated the Tenth Doctor?

Daleks – 2005 onwards 2

1. Who calls himself the God of all Daleks?
2. Who does the Supreme Dalek refer to as 'the Abomination'?
3. Who destroys the first revived 'stone' Dalek in the National Museum?
4. What colour is the Eternal Dalek?
5. What does the Eleventh Doctor hit an Ironside Dalek with, to try to provoke it?

6. What is contained in the Progenitor?
7. Why wouldn't the Progenitor recognise the Daleks until they had the Doctor's testimony?
8. What common feature is shared by all the Daleks confined to 'intensive care' on the Dalek Asylum?
9. What does Oswin do upon hacking into the Daleks' path web?
10. What do the Daleks use to take the TARDIS to the Crucible?

*

11. What energy is at the heart of the Dalek Crucible?
12. What bullets, loaded in the Game Station guards' guns, does Captain Jack say will be enough to blow a Dalek wide open?
13. What does the Metacrisis Doctor build to destroy Davros and the Daleks?
14. Who does the Eleventh Doctor refer to as 'the little Daleks'?
15. What Dalek-related bedtime story does the Eleventh Doctor tell George he loved?

Davros 1

1. The Fifth Doctor tells Davros he is not on the space station as his prisoner, but as his – what?
2. Which employee of Tranquil Repose does Davros have transferred to his personal staff?
3. What part of Davros is shot off by Bostock?
4. How is Davros known on Necros?
5. What does Davros tell the Fourth Doctor must be accomplished before he can allow himself the luxury of death?

6. Who is the first person Davros 'recruits' on the space station?
7. Who does Kara hire to kill Davros?
8. What is to happen to Davros after his defeat on Necros?
9. What position does Davros offer the Fifth Doctor?
10. What does Kara say she would willingly sell if it would help Davros's cause?

*

11. Where are Davros's laboratories in Tranquil Repose?
12. What 'species type' is Davros, according to the Movellans?
13. What is to happen to Davros at the end of *Destiny of the Daleks*?
14. Who does the Fourth Doctor accuse Davros of misquoting?
15. How long is Davros frozen before the events of *Resurrection of the Daleks*?

Davros 2

1. Who rescues Davros from the Time War?
2. What is each of post-Time War Davros's new Daleks grown from?
3. What weapon does Davros create to destroy 'every single corner of creation' and leave Daleks the only life forms in existence?
4. Seeing who on board the Crucible leads Davros to declare that the circle of time is closing?
5. Which member of the Kaled Scientific Elite tries to organise a movement against Davros?

6. What does Davros plan to turn into a source of unimaginable power using the Hand of Omega?
7. Whose jaws does the Doctor see Davros's command ship fly into during the Time War?
8. On the Crucible, who does Davros accuse of betraying the Daleks?
9. How long can Davros survive with his life-support systems switched off?
10. At Tranquil Repose, Davros turns people of status and ambition into Daleks – what happens to the rest?

11. Where does the Doctor witness Davros's death in the first year of the Time War (or so he thinks)?
12. On the Crucible, who does the Supreme Dalek say are now 'playthings of Davros'?
13. What does Davros say the Doctor takes and fashions into weapons?
14. What name does Davros bestow on the Tenth Doctor 'for ever'?
15. What can be found in a cave at the edge of the Wasteland on Skaro?

Prehistoric Monsters!

1. Which dinosaur does a newly regenerated Doctor tell the Brigadier is 'large and placid. And stupid'?
2. Which reptilian race keeps a dinosaur, described by the Brigadier as 'a subterranean Loch Ness Monster', as a pet?
3. Which of the Doctor's companions dies in the space-freighter crash that also wipes out the dinosaurs?
4. What nickname does the Doctor give to the Triceratops he tries to ride?
5. What dinosaur do the Doctor and Jo encounter inside the Miniscope?

6. Which dinosaur does the Sixth Doctor say will 'bite your leg off, chew it all up, bone and all, all in one go'?
7. The arrival of which dinosaur allows the Doctor and Sarah Jane to escape from a detention-centre transport?
8. What does Brian throw to get the Triceratops to 'fetch'?
9. What, according to a sign in Hyde Park in *The Wedding of River Song*, are 'vermin' and not to be fed?
10. Who thinks there are dinosaurs at the centre of the Earth?

*

11. What does the hunter Riddell say he wants more than anything?
12. Ace tells the Doctor that she loves dinosaurs – but what does she say she hates?
13. Which of these dinosaurs does the Eleventh Doctor not encounter on board the Ark: (a) Spinosaurus, (b) Velociraptor or (c) Ankylosaurus?
14. Who wants to return to the Cretaceous Age and realise the potential of the dinosaurs?
15. What coloured map pin represents a Pterodactyl according to Sergeant Benton's colour code?

Mythical Monsters 1 – Vampires

1. How are Aukon, Camilla and Zargo collectively known?
2. In which city do the Doctor, Rory and Amy encounter 'vampires'?
3. What sort of blood-drinking alien is hiding at the Royal Hope Hospital?
4. What creatures do *Homo sapiens* evolve into that have an insatiable hunger for blood?
5. Who is the first of the Chosen Ones, selected by Aukon to be turned into a vampire?

6. After the war with the Time Lords, the King Vampire vanished from time and space. Where did it really go?
7. Why is Rosanna transforming girls into vampires?
8. K-9's folklore section contains vampire lore from how many inhabited planets?
9. What do the Time Lords discover is the only way to kill a great vampire?
10. What creatures are, according to the Doctor, 'not vampires. Fish from space'?

*

11. According to Aukon, what have they fed to the Great One as well as blood?
12. What story was originally called 'The Vampire from Space'?
13. For what 1996 event was a robot Dracula an attraction?
14. Which creatures that the Fourth Doctor meets absorb blood to feed on the globulin it contains?
15. What does the Eleventh Doctor use to hold back the 'vampires' he meets in 1560?

Mythical Monsters 2 – Werewolves

1. Who calls Mags his 'rare specimen'?
2. Who transforms into the werewolf-like 'antiman'?
3. Who is the first person to transform into a werewolf-like Primord?
4. What do the Brethren from the Glen of St Catherine wear so the werewolf won't attack them?
5. What does the Koh-i-Nor magnify to destroy the werewolf?

6. What 'mutation of the blood' do Queen Victoria and her descendants suffer from?
7. Who, along with Robert MacLeish's father, planned a trap for the werewolf?
8. What planet does Mags come from?
9. What makes Mags transform in the circus ring?
10. What would bring about the Empire of the Wolf in the nineteenth century?

*

11. Who do the Doctor and Peri suspect of being a Lycanthrope?
12. In what year does a 'shooting star' bring the werewolf curse to Scotland?
13. What non-Werewolf does the Brigadier kill with silver bullets?
14. What is the Doctor's technical description of the Werewolf he meets in Scotland?
15. What is imbedded in the doors of the MacLeish home to keep werewolves at bay?

Mythical Monsters 3 – Minotaur

1. What phrase do the God Complex Minotaur's victims repeat?
2. What maze-like structure do the Nimon live in?
3. The story of the Minotaur inspires which companion to mark a path with an unravelled cardigan?
4. What does the Eleventh Doctor initially believe the God Complex's Minotaur feeds on?
5. What does Zoe say to make the Land of Fiction Minotaur disappear?

6. What is guarded by the Atlantean Minotaur?
7. What part of a Nimon doubled as an energy weapon?
8. What does the Eleventh Doctor destroy, allowing the Minotaur to die?
9. What do the Nimon call their movement from planet to planet?
10. Who is killed saving Jo Grant from the Minotaur?

*

11. What does Romana find in Number Four Hold, with a label on it reading 'To the Doctor. A souvenir with love and thanks for all his help with the Minotaur. Theseus and Ariadne'?
12. What crystalline tribute is demanded by the Nimon?
13. According to Darius, what wish did his friend make that saw him transformed into the Minotaur?
14. In what story does the Doctor see Amy's drawing of a Minotaur?
15. The spa in which the Eleventh Doctor traps the Minotaur is named after which cursed relative of the mythical Minotaur?

Monsters and Aliens – The 1960s

1. Which companion is nearly turned into a Fish Person?
2. What happens if the Celestial Toymaker loses a game?
3. Who are the gods of the Optera?
4. Which of the Sensorites' senses is particularly sensitive?
5. Who was the commanding officer of the Drahvins that the First Doctor met?

6. What sort of power feeds the Krotons' dynatrope?
7. What gas do the Rills breathe?
8. What planet do the Visians inhabit?
9. What robots see the world through a hexagonal viewpoint?
10. Who invented WOTAN?

11. What creatures once lived in the slime at the bottom of the ocean on Aridius?
12. Who has a Yeti in his museum?
13. What caused the Chameleons to lose their identities?
14. What name is given to the giant bats of Desperus?
15. What destroys the Weed Creature's nerve centre?

Monsters and Aliens – The 1970s

1. Which race destroys its failures, such as Atlantis?
2. Who does the Doctor describe as a hermaphrodite hexapod?
3. How many splinters has Scaroth split into?
4. What creatures can travel along broadcast wavelengths of any sort?
5. What 'thinking molecule' is offered as payment by the Axons?

6. What planet is home to a race of mining engineers?
7. Which employee of Harrison Chase turns into a Krynoid?
8. Who are the leaders the opposing factions of Vogans at the time of the Doctor's visit?
9. What are Usurians listed under in Professor Thripsted's Flora and Fauna of the Universe?
10. When does the Doctor think Mandragora might once again cause trouble for the Earth?

*

11. Ten of what creature can 'strip the flesh from a man's arm almost before he can cry out'?
12. How long have Nestenes been colonising other planets for, according to Channing?
13. What is removed from Arcturus's life-support system in a supposed attempt on his life?
14. Where do Drashigs come from?
15. Who gives the Sea Devils their name?

Monsters and Aliens – The 1980s

1. Who is the leader of the Bannermen?
2. What teleporting creatures look like black cats?
3. What race does Monarch belong to?
4. Who plans to explode a sun to scatter his race's eggs?
5. What is the Androgum term for the bloodline each belongs to?

6. Who is a representative of the Galatron Mining Corporation?
7. Which Eternal is fascinated by Tegan?
8. What gas is toxic to Mogarians?
9. What is Kane's gaoler in Iceworld?
10. Who created the Kandyman?

11. What creatures does the Doctor say are made from random particles from the atmosphere?
12. What does the Doctor use to destroy the Myrka?
13. On what planet are Voltrox found?
14. What type of plant is Meglos?
15. What came to Earth on board a Hakol probe?

Monsters and Aliens – 2005–2009

1. What did the Abzorbaloff call himself while in human form?
2. What creatures are made from living fat?
3. What does the Master name after something from Gallifreyan fairy tales?
4. What alien race colonised Messaline alongside the humans?
5. What body part does Ood Operations remove from each Ood?

6. What monster did the Doctor trap using 'home video'?
7. How long is the Family of Blood's usual lifespan?
8. The Weeping Angels used to be called what, according to the Doctor?
9. What is Bannakaffalatta's secret?
10. By what name did Lady Eddison know her Vespiform lover?

*

11. By what name does the Editor call the Mighty Jagrafess?
12. What aren't Trees of the Forest of Cheem supposed to show in public?
13. What creatures might a disobedient Slitheen family member be fed to?
14. Humans of what blood type are controlled by the Sycorax during their invasion?
15. When the Doctor last met the Krillitanes prior to their arrival at Deffry Vale, they had looked human apart from what one difference?

Monsters and Aliens – 2010 onwards

1. What species was Nephew?
2. What substance are Gangers made from?
3. What race owned the Space Ark that Solomon hijacked?
4. What eyeless beings work for the Great Intelligence?
5. What monster was 'Handles' once a part of?

6. What creatures are part human, part Smiler?
7. Who turned members of his own race into cyborgs in order to win a war?
8. What does Alexei call Miss Kizlet's 'servers'?
9. What was once the most virulent enemy of the Silurians?
10. What is it a Level One Heresy to do to a Headless Monk?

11. What order does the Doctor make the Silence give to everyone who watches the Moon landing?
12. What are the 'pest controllers of the universe' according to Gallifreyan myth?
13. What cybernetic insects does the Doctor encounter on Hedgewick's World?
14. For whom is the Pyramid of the Rings of Akhaten a holy site?
15. In what painting does the Doctor spot the Krafayis?

A Policy of Non-Intervention

1. What sentence is the Doctor given for breaking the Time Lord law of non-interference in the affairs of other planets?
2. What is the secret known only to the Time Lords and the Sisterhood of Karn?
3. What planet do the Time Lords send the Doctor to, to deliver a box of tablets?
4. What did Rassilon forbid the use of when he sealed off the Death Zone?
5. What device was used by Time Lords to customise stars?

6. What entertainment device was banned by the Time Lords, with all examples called in and destroyed?
7. Who broke into the Matrix to steal its information, working from a base on Earth?
8. Whose discovery means the course of natural evolution throughout the universe will be affected, leading to the Time Lords having him killed – or so the Doctor is told?
9. What does Borusa think will throw the Time Lords back to the darkest age if it's used?
10. What punishment do the Time Lords visit on the War Lord?

*

11. What prison ship do the Time Lords create to hold Dalek prisoners during the Time War?
12. Who thought of the Time Lords as gods, before warring among themselves and destroying their own planet?
13. What did Mawdryn and his colleagues steal from Gallifrey to try to turn themselves into Time Lords?
14. What did Omega create as the ultimate defence for Gallifrey?
15. What did the Time Lords use to draw the Earth and its constellation billions of miles across space?

Cybermen – The 1960s 1

1. What 'weakness' has been removed from the Cybermen's brains?
2. What happens to the Cybermen when Mondas 'melts'?
3. Why is the injured Jamie of no value to the Cybermen?
4. How much does Kaftan offer to the first man to open the doors of the Cyber city?
5. Where does the Doctor discover Cybermen are hiding on the Moonbase?

6. What is the cause of the sudden air pressure drops experienced by the Moonbase?
7. Who is the leader of the expedition to Telos?
8. What do the Cybermen plan to do with the Gravitron?
9. Why do the Cybermen think it irrelevant when Polly asks if they wouldn't care about someone in pain?
10. How long were the Cybermen frozen on Telos before the expedition arrived, according to the Doctor?

*

11. What nickname does Ben give the Cyberman he kills with its own weapon?
12. What weapon does General Cutler plan to use against Mondas?
13. What does Ben discover the Cybermen are afraid of?
14. Who is murdered by the Cybermen while collecting supplies from the Moonbase food store?
15. What do the Cybermen infect the Moonbase's sugar with?

Cybermen – The 1960s 2

1. Cybermen are shown climbing down the steps from which London landmark?
2. The induction of which emotion by Vaughn causes a Cyberman to go mad?
3. Where do the *Invasion* Cybermen recognise the Doctor and Jamie from?
4. Who is the leader of the Cybermen on Telos?
5. Who do the Telos Cybermen plan to make the leader of the new race of Cybermen?

6. What do the Telos Cybermats home in on, according to the Doctor?
7. What does Duggan call his 'pet' Cybermat?
8. Gemma Corwyn sacrifices her life to get what message to the Doctor?
9. What is used on the Wheel to clog the Cybermen's chest units?
10. What invention of Professor Watkins' does Tobias Vaughn use as a weapon against the Cybermen?

*

11. Who is the first UNIT soldier to be killed by a Cyberman?
12. How long has Tobias Vaughn been planning the invasion of Earth with the Cybermen?
13. What lighting system is used inside the Cyber city on Telos?
14. What important substance do the Cybermats 'consume' on the Wheel?
15. What does the Doctor use to destroy Cybermats on the Wheel?

Cybermen – The 1970s and 1980s

1. What physical characteristic distinguishes *Revenge of the Cybermen*'s Cyberleader from the other Cybermen?
2. What does Ace use to attack the Cybermen?
3. What new Cyber rank can be found in the credits of *Earthshock*?
4. Who assists the Cybermen in locating Voga?
5. What do Lady Peinforte and Richard use to kill Cybermen?

6. What do the Cyberman plan to use to destroy Earth before 1986?
7. How are Nerva's crew infected with the Cyber poison?
8. Where does Lytton discover the Cybermen have a ship hidden?
9. Which escaped member of the Telos work party disguises himself as a Cyberman?
10. Which particular Cyberman did the Sixth Doctor think had been destroyed in a previous encounter?

*

11. In *Silver Nemesis,* who pretends to betray his leader and asks the Cybermen to make him one of them?
12. Who kills the Cyber Leader and saves the Seventh Doctor's life?
13. Which member of Captain Briggs's crew is working for the Cybermen?
14. What is the purpose of the Earth conference the Cybermen are trying to prevent?
15. Which two specific previous adventures does the Cyber Leader reference in *Earthshock*?

Cybermen – 2005 onwards

1. Where does the Ninth Doctor come across a Cyber relic?
2. Who created the Cyberman in 'Pete's World'?
3. What occasion do the Cybermen gatecrash in *Rise of the Cybermen*?
4. Who bars the way of the Cybermen as they try to retreat to the breach in Torchwood Tower?
5. Who calls the Cybermen her 'knights in shining armour'?

6. Who is turned into a Cyberman the night before her wedding?
7. Who is in charge of collecting homeless people and 'upgrading' them into Cybermen?
8. What breaks down the barriers between worlds, allowing the Cybermen to cross from the alternative universe?
9. How many Cybermen will be awakened from Hedgewick's World?
10. What happens when a Cyber Leader is destroyed?

*

11. In the cellar of what address did Jackson Lake find the Cybermen?
12. What part of a Cyberman does the Doctor scramble the circuits of in the Underhenge?
13. In *Nightmare in Silver*, what term is used for the collective of all Cybermen?
14. What does the Cyber-Doctor suggest he might call himself instead of 'Cyberplanner'?
15. What adjective do the Cybermen use to describe Dalek design?

The Master – The 1970s 1

1. Who is the first onscreen person to be shrunk by the Master?
2. Who does the Master plan to sacrifice to Azal?
3. What does the Keller Machine reveal as the Master's greatest fear?
4. What does the Master's TARDIS disguise itself as when he first arrives on Earth?
5. Who does the Master pretend to be when he arrives on Uxarieus?

6. The Master's invocation of Azal is really which nursery rhyme said backwards?
7. At the end of *Terror of the Autons*, who does Captain Yates shoot, thinking it's the Master?
8. Who was the Master's assistant when the Keller Machine was installed at Stangmoor?
9. Who does the Master lead to Earth in return for the death of the Doctor and the destruction of all life on the planet?
10. In what episode of *Colony in Space* does the Master first appear?

*

11. What country is 'Emil Keller' supposedly from?
12. What does the Doctor take from the Master in *Terror of the Autons*, which the Master regains in *The Mind of Evil*?
13. Who is sent from Washington to deal with the Master?
14. According to the Master, what is a basic rule of life?
15. Who does the Master replace as vicar of Devil's End?

The Master – The 1970s 2

1. Who are Professor Thascales's two assistants?
2. What allies does the Master refer to as 'great lumbering idiots'?
3. What is the first sign the Doctor finds that indicates the Master is on Gallifrey?
4. What are all the men at the Master's island prison immune to, according to Trenchard?
5. Who thinks the Master has 'the bearing of the gods'?

6. What does the Master ask Trenchard for, 'for the bedroom'?
7. How did the Master learn about the Sea Devils?
8. What book does the Master read while travelling to the planet of the Ogrons?
9. What happens when Jo trips the alarm beam in the Master's TARDIS?
10. When the Master talks to Azal about his strong leadership, which two historical figures does the Doctor compare him to?

*

11. In which subject is the Master 'almost up to the Doctor's standard' – or so the Doctor tells Spandrell?
12. On what planet did Goth meet the Master?
13. Who accuses Professor Thascales of being a charlatan?
14. In *Frontier in Space*, the Master pretends to be a commissioner from which planet?
15. What does the Doctor say the Master would postpone an execution to do?

The Master – The 1980s

1. What creature's form does the Master's TARDIS take on Traken?
2. In *Castrovalva*, which member of the TARDIS crew does the Master kidnap?
3. Who does the Master use to impersonate King John?
4. What form does the Master's TARDIS take in thirteenth-century England?
5. Who is the first Doctor the Master encounters in the Death Zone?

6. What disguise does the Master adopt in *Castrovalva*?
7. What form does the Master's TARDIS take in *Castrovalva*?
8. On prehistoric Earth, what does the Master 'melt down' to use as a store of protoplasm?
9. What do the Time Lord Inner Council offer the Master in return for his rescuing the Doctor?
10. What monsters does the Master temporarily ally himself with in the Death Zone?

*

11. What does Flavia give the Master so he can convince the Doctor of his good faith?
12. Which embodiment of the Xeraphin sides with the Master?
13. What component does Peri take from the TARDIS to prevent the Master using it?
14. What (fake) TARDIS component does the Master give the Doctor at the Pharos Project to demonstrate his trust?
15. In what story does the Master first use the term 'tissue compression eliminator'?

The Master – The 1980s and 1990s

1. What description does Squeak use for the Master?
2. What are the Master's last words to the Doctor on Sarn?
3. Whose body does the Master take over in San Francisco, 1999?
4. What colour are the Cheetah-Master's eyes?
5. Which two 'star witnesses' does the Master send to the Doctor's trial?

6. In what does the Master leave nineteenth-century Earth?
7. What substance on Sarn does the Master use to restore himself to his original size?
8. What planet did the Master visit before following the Rani to Earth?
9. Who does the Master take control of with one of the Rani's 'sweetmeats'?
10. What does the Master have a 'very good copy' of, enabling him to enter the Matrix?

*

11. What historical figure does the Master tell Chang Lee was really the Doctor?
12. What is the Master's TARDIS disguised as, inside the Matrix?
13. Why does the Rani stop the Master killing Peri?
14. What does the Doctor use to attack the Master in the ambulance, so he and Grace can escape?
15. What was used to trap the Master at the end of *The Ultimate Foe*?

The Master – 2005 onwards

1. Who finally kills the Master?
2. What does Naismith want the Master to repair?
3. Who shoots the Master on Malcassairo, causing his regeneration?
4. Who draws Yana's attention to his perception-filtered fob watch?
5. Apart from Wilf, who is the only human on Earth not to turn into a member of 'the Master race'?

6. Why did the Time Lords resurrect the Master?
7. Who does the Master plan to kill first to mark his rocket fleet being ready to launch?
8. Why do the Time Lords implant the sound of drums in the Master's head?
9. Who takes the Master's ring from his funeral pyre?
10. What does the Master turn the Doctor's TARDIS into to allow the Toclafane invasion?

*

11. Where was Yana found as a child?
12. Who does the Master call an 'ugly, fat-faced bunch of wet, snivelling traitors'?
13. What sports award did Saxon supposedly gain at Cambridge?
14. Who is the first person the Master orders the Toclafane to kill?
15. What is the first *Doctor Who* story to reference Harold Saxon?

Anagrams 1

Solve the anagrams to find alien individuals or monstrous beasts encountered by the Doctor and his friends:

1. Mark Y
2. Goner
3. Dog Rage
4. Soul Is
5. Cheesy Bard

6. Gas Mat Beam
7. Grave Primate
8. Ask Fairy
9. Red Oyster
10. Wash Later

11. Laser Net
12. Angular Cab Kid
13. Tell Egg Incinerate
14. Seen Sunset Concession
15. Parachute Nail

Anagrams 2

Solve the anagrams to find monsters or aliens encountered by the Doctor and his friends:

1. Elves Aid
2. Arson Ant
3. Scary Ox
4. Literal Ink
5. Pram Loaves

6. Mercy Bat
7. Darn Elm
8. Erotic Rain
9. Carrot Tat
10. Star Van Ahead

11. Vagrant Pal
12. Sea Snark
13. Tramp One
14. Same Biter
15. Duke Fir Nut

Anagrams 3

Solve the anagrams to find monsters or aliens encountered by the Doctor and his friends:

1. Domino
2. Ice Lens
3. Grot
4. A Lark
5. Olive Pry

6. Sunny Rate
7. Good Strap
8. Room Heave
9. Ache Lemon
10. Soda Pie

11. Eat Falcon
12. Hex Darling Aroma
13. Pat Salmon
14. Elf Hand
15. Pawn Negligee

Anagrams 4

Solve the anagrams to find alien races encountered by the Doctor and his friends:

1. Corny
2. Halt
3. Resist One
4. Canon Raid
5. Nail Soon

6. Ruin Sail
7. Rice Air Row
8. Lard Bin
9. Rain Aid
10. Eel Rant

11. River Toot
12. Rat Sermon
13. Ruin USA
14. Thy Nation
15. Faun Rise

Closing Credits (4)

Initially – W

1. What W is the alien who steals faces through television sets?
2. What W are insect-like creatures found on the Ark in Space?
3. What W is the colour of the robots met by Jamie and Zoe in the Land of Fiction?
4. What W are the stone angels encountered by Sally Sparrow?
5. What W is the Racnoss's spaceship?

6. What W is Trinity, who frequently reports on alien happenings on Earth?
7. What W is the moor where the Silurians are found?
8. What W is the sort of creature the Doctor plans to use to erase Clara's memory?
9. What W was the Doctor all the time?
10. What W is an enthusiastic fan of the Psychic Circus?

*

11. What W is the doctor who was a childhood friend of the Scarmans?
12. What W does Madge Arwell turn out not to be, thanks to the Doctor?
13. What W draw graffiti on the corridors of Paradise Towers?
14. What W is the man Rose is looking for when she first meets the Doctor?
15. What W is the Spiridon who saved Jo's life?

Initially – QXY

1. What Q are robot servants of the cruel Dominators?
2. What Y is leader of the alien Voord?
3. What Y are the Great Intelligence's furry robot servants?
4. What X is the computer that went insane after the Doctor 'fixed' it?
5. What Q are the marks on the Seventh Doctor's jumper?

6. What Q is the first human to come into contact with the Wenley Moor Silurians?
7. What X is queen of the Pirate Planet?
8. What X is the planet where the Space Museum could be found?
9. What Y is the naked child found on the coast of the Silver Devastation with only a fob watch?
10. What Q is the most important thing for Jackson and the crew of the R1C?

*

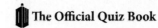

11. What X encountered by the Fifth Doctor have absorbed their whole race into a single bioplasmic body?
12. What Y does the Doctor use to take a gravity reading on the Ark in Space?
13. What Q is a name given to the Doctor by Miss Hawthorne?
14. What Q is a planet in the Fourth Universe, once visited by the Doctor and Susan?
15. What X is the subject of Kane's ice statue?

Initially – Z

1. What Z are antlike aliens controlled by the Animus?
2. What Z is the god the Doctor is mistaken for in Ancient Greece?
3. What Z are shapechanging aliens who take forms including Harry Sullivan and Queen Elizabeth I?
4. What Z is the companion who thinks the Doctor is almost as clever as she is?
5. What Z is the professor who declares that nothing in the world can stop him now?

6. What Z is Trine-E's fellow robot presenter?
7. What Z is the swordmaster who serves Prince Reynart?
8. What Z is the Pirate Planet?
9. What Z is the race to which Bannakaffalatta belongs?
10. What Z is possessed archaeologist Toby?

*

11. What Z is a beef-flavoured drink found on Satellite Five?
12. What Z is the energy that powers Magnus Greel's Time Cabinet?
13. What Z had a brother who suffered from robophobia?
14. What Z is an Ice Warrior met by the Second Doctor and Victoria?
15. What Z is Mels's surname?

Next-Time Trailer

Missing Vowels 1 – Story Titles

1. THRK
2. FRNTS
3. CLSNGTM
4. THNVSN
5. FRHR

6. THCWRRRS
7. PLNTFVL
8. MYSCHC
9. VLTNFTHDLKS
10. THSDSFDTH

11. THLTMTF
12. TP
13. TMNDTHRN
14. PLNTFTHD
15. THFRSFPMP

Missing Vowels 2 – Episode Titles

1. THDGFDSTRCTN
2. THVLVTWB
3. NFRN
4. RLCK
5. NNRTHLYCHLD

6. THDTHFDCTRWH
7. CRSS
8. SCPTDNGR
9. THCLSTLTYRM
10. THWKNGLLY

11. THKCRRL
12. CHNGFDNTTY
13. THRDL
14. THNWLLNGWRRRS
15. SSSSNTPKNG

Gold Run

Identify the following from their initial letters:

1. NNY – City on New Earth
2. SSS – Organisation to which Sara Kingdom belongs
3. HM – A religious order whose members rarely lowered their hoods
4. JTR – Serial killer allegedly eaten by Madame Vastra
5. VN – The 'piranhas of the air' who live in the books of The Library

6. FOC – Tree people who visit Platform One to witness Earthdeath
7. COA – Object stolen by Lady Christina de Souza
8. COTFG –Augmented Androgum chatelaine
9. FW – Device inside which John Smith's real persona is hidden
10. TOL – Landmark under which UNIT HQ is located

*

11. SK – Room where food is prepared on the Ark
12. MJOTHHM – Alien found on Floor 500 of Satellite Five
13. MGHTUADC – Establishment that offers degrees in Earthonomics
14. BWM – Game show loved by the Ninth Doctor
15. BPG – Reference work including information on Ribos

Adding a Bit 1

1. What precedes Scoop, Agency, Ram?
2. What precedes Devil, Base, Beggar?
3. What precedes Orchid, Guardian, Hole?
4. What precedes Bat, Thalira, Victoria?
5. What precedes Lance, Pen, Screwdriver?

6. What precedes Carrier, Devastation, Nemesis?
7. What precedes Games, Machine, Doctor?
8. What precedes One, Healer, Intelligence?
9. What precedes Circus, Pollen, Paper?
10. What precedes Man, Mat, Planner?

11. What precedes 79, Ten, Shaw?
12. What precedes Blade, Pike, Knight?
13. What precedes Clown, Caretaker, Engineer?
14. What precedes Escape, Maker, Mountain?
15. What precedes Robber, Probe, Parasite?

Adding a Bit 2

1. What follows Human, Dalek, Armageddon?
2. What follows Time, Cold, Trojan?
3. What follows Final, Lazarus, Sontaran?
4. What follows Wenley, Stang, Tullock?
5. What follows Inter, Zeta, Androzani?

6. What follows Impossible, Pirate, Tenth?
7. What follows Servo, White, Raston Warrior?
8. What follows Pipe, Cheetah, Almost?
9. What follows Gabriel, Harrison, 'You all's in a'?
10. What follows Brendon, Farringham, Deffry Vale High?

11. What follows Steel, Poison, Mr Blue?
12. What follows Journey's, World's, Devil's?
13. What follows Z, Reality, Cyber?
14. What follows Moon, Sea, Bowie?
15. What follows Time, Unwilling, Ice?

Adding a Bit 3

What word can be put inbetween the words below to create two separate *Doctor Who*-related words or terms?

1. Bad ____ weed
2. Oncoming _____ cage
3. Long ____ Station
4. Flesh ____ lash
5. Hand of ____ Her

6. Green _____ Zone
7. Grand _____ Tavannes
8. King's _____ Run
9. Glitter ___ fighters
10. Cyber _____ Clent

11. Terra _____ Centauri
12. Old _____ Bloodtide
13. Wooden ____ Rokon
14. Time ____ master
15. Dragon ____ maker

Quote Unquote

Each linked pair includes quotations from two different stories –
can you identify them?

1. 'Have you met Miss Smith? She's my best friend.' (The
   Doctor) / 'Really, do you think I'd leave my best friend
   without a defence mechanism?' (The Doctor)
2. 'Wonderful chap. All of them.' (The Brigadier)' / 'Wonderful
   chap. Both of him.' (The Brigadier)
3. 'Look me in the eye, pull the trigger, end my life.' (The
   Doctor) / 'Come then, look me in the eye, end my life.' (to the
   Doctor)
4. 'What you need is a jolly good smacked bottom.' (The
   Doctor) / 'Just you watch your lip or I'll put you across my
   knee and larrup you.' (Jamie)
5. 'You're a beautiful woman, probably…' (The Doctor) / 'I'm a
   Sagittarius, probably.' (The Doctor)

6. 'You're just a pathetic bunch of tin soldiers skulking about
   the galaxy in an ancient spaceship.' (The Doctor) / 'Time
   was, four Daleks could've conquered the world. But instead
   you're skulking away, hidden in the dark, experimenting.'
   (The Doctor)

7. 'Nine hundred years of time and space, I've never met anyone who wasn't important.' (The Doctor) / 'I mean, you're not special, you're not powerful, you're not connected, you're not clever, you're not important…' (The Doctor)

8. 'I'll never eat oysters again.' (Sarah) / 'I'll never be cruel to an electron in a particle accelerator again.' (The Doctor)

9. 'Place of origin?' 'Gallifrey.' 'Ireland?' 'Oh, I expect so.' (about the Doctor) / 'Where did you learn to draw?' 'Gallifrey.' 'Is that in Ireland?' 'Yes. It must be, yes.' (The Doctor)

10. 'Promises to aliens have no validity.' (Cyber Leader) / 'Cybermen do not promise. Such ideas have no value.' (Cyberman)

11. 'We'll all become unpeople doing unthings untogether.' (The Doctor) / 'Nothing happened. A sort of unexplosion has taken place.' (The Doctor)

12. 'I've got a lantern and a pair of waders, and possibly the most fearsome piece of hand artillery in all England. What could possibly go wrong?' (The Doctor) / 'All I've got to do is pass as an ordinary human being. Simple. What could possibly go wrong?' (The Doctor)

13. 'Sad really, isn't it? People spend all their time making nice things, and other people come along and break them.' (The Doctor) / 'Why can't people be nice to one another, just for a change. I mean, I'm an alien, and you don't want to drag me into a swamp, do you?' (The Doctor)

14. 'If we fight like animals, we die like animals!' (The Doctor) / 'Do you want to end your lives fighting like animals?' (The

Doctor)

15. 'Never trust a man as wears a hat.' (about the Doctor) / 'I've never seen him go for food like this before. It's usually hats.' (about the Doctor)

Two's Company

1. Which story features both a Doctor-to-be and a companion-to-be?
2. In which two stories is the TARDIS's HADS enabled?
3. Which two Doctors face Autons in their debut stories?
4. Which two adjacent stories feature parent / offspring acting teams (one of whom is a Doctor or companion)?
5. The Third Doctor didn't encounter the Cybermen until *The Five Doctors,* but in which two Third Doctor stories are they briefly seen?

6. Which two established comedy double acts have appeared as pairs of characters in *Doctor Who*?
7. Which two episodes of *Doctor Who* have been remounted?
8. In which two stories is a dropped drinking vessel seen to become whole again?
9. Which are the only two stories to have numerals in their titles?
10. Which two villains does the Doctor kill with cyanide?

11. Which two Doctors have been sentenced to a lunar penal colony?
12. In which two consecutive stories do we hear the Second

Doctor's thoughts?

13. Which two companions are alluded to in the story directly before each makes a first appearance?
14. Which are the only two stories to credit Nicholas Courtney as 'The Brigadier'?
15. Which acclaimed actress has appeared in *Doctor Who* twice – once in the 1970s and once in the 1980s – but does not interact with the Doctor in either role?

Connect 3

What connects:

1.   The First Doctor, Ian, Rebec?
2.   Omega, Alpha, Beta?
3.   *The Ark, Inferno, The End of the World?*
4.   Secret book, Oscar Botcherby, Eldred?
5.   Sea Devil, Solonian Mutant, Drashig?

6.   Fred, Taffy, Malone?
7.   *The Web of Fear, Fury from the Deep, The Wheel in Space?*
8.   Lee Richards, Maggy Armitage, Yvonne Gallagher?
9.   'Mary Had a Little Lamb', 'Humpty Dumpty', 'See Saw Margery Daw'?
10. Barbara in *The Web Planet*, Nyssa in *Logopolis*, Tegan in *The Visitation*?

11. Malpha, Chicki, Jamie?
12. Stag's head, dartboard, a bowl of fruit?
13. Annabelle, Bernice, Madame de Pompadour?
14. Nyssa, Leela, Victoria?
15. A Didonian creature, a Zarbi, the Rills' servants?

Connect 4

What connects:

1. *The Mind Robber, Castrovalva, Forest of the Dead, Amy's Choice*?
2. Voga, Sir Keith, Usher, Murray?
3. Handbots, Grandma Connolly, Auton policeman, Cybermen's androids?
4. Scaroth, Meglos, the Tenth Doctor, the Face of Boe?
5. Senora Camara, Mrs Trefusis, Lady Morgana Montcalm, the Mother Superior of the Convent of the Little Sisters of Saint Gudula?

6. Grun, Ascaris, Kemel, Cyclops?
7. *Carnival of Monsters, The Green Death, Planet of the Spiders, Hide*?
8. James Stirling, W.G. Grace, Land of Fiction computer, Daleks' plan?
9. Vicki, Polly, Mel, Ace?
10. Channing, Chang Lee, Lady Jennifer, Tegan?

*

11. The Daleks, the Solonians, Mawdryn's companions, Ken Barker?
12. The Trojan Wars, the Dark Ages, the American War of Independence, the Luddite riots?
13. An Ogron, Sarah in *The Hand of Fear*, Peri in *The Two Doctors*, Reverend Matthews?
14. *The Christmas Invasion, The Runaway Bride, Turn Left, The Power of Three?*
15. Triangle, bisected circle, trident, crescent?

Connect 5

What connects:

1. Scaroth, Monoid, Spiridon plants, Quillam, a well on Segonax?
2. Scarecrow, vicar, knight, sorcerer, paramedic?
3. Red, blue, orange, yellow, white?
4. The Savages, the Gonds, the Macra-threatened colonists, the Ogrons, the servants of the Three Who Rule?
5. Boat, Farm, Grave, Rail, Stack?

6. Clara, the Second Doctor, Bellboy, Room 214, Bing Crosby?
7. Proverb, spearmint, hopscotch, lullaby, feet?
8. Amazonia, Primords, Dukkha, Old Mother, Kriz?
9. Crimean War, American Civil War, Boer War, English Civil War, 1917?
10. The Abzorbaloff, Steven Taylor, Teka, *Aliens of London*, Creet?

*

11. Brus, Zil, Gidi, Ranx, Darp?
12. Sand Beast, Gel Guards, Technix, Whomobile, Ice Lord?
13. Sarah in *The Android Invasion*, Susan in *The Five Doctors*, Susan in *The Dalek Invasion of Earth*, Vicki in *Galaxy 4*, Romana in *The Androids of Tara*?
14. *Planet of Giants, The Mind Robber, The Dominators, Resurrection of the Daleks, Terror of the Zygons*?
15. Steven, Dodo, Victoria, Zoe, Katarina?

What Comes Next?

What comes next in the following sequences?

1. Jethrik, Calufrax, the Great Seal of Diplos?
2. Trees, the Moxx of Balhoon, Adherents of the Repeated Meme?
3. *The Daleks, The Dalek Invasion of Earth, The Space Museum?*
4. Matt Smith, Peter Davison, David Tennant?
5. Fez, top hat, Santa hat?

6. Harriet Jones, Jabe, Controller?
7. *An Unearthly Child, Planet of Giants, The Chase?*
8. *The Ambassadors of Death, Colony in Space, The Curse of Peladon?*
9. *The Smugglers, The War Games, Inferno?*
10. Exterminated, exterminated, shot by Chen?

11. *An Unearthly Child, The Masque of Mandragora, The Leisure Hive?*
12. *The Keys of Marinus* Episodes 3 and 4, *The Aztecs* Episodes 2 and 3, *The Sensorites* Episodes 4 and 5?
13. *Marco Polo, The Dalek Invasion of Earth, The Web Planet?*
14. Earth, Kembel, Peladon?
15. Macra, Zygons, Silurians?

Titles Within Titles 1

Can you identify the stories in which these post-2005 story titles crop up in pre-1996 dialogue?

1. 'I am not a student of **Human Nature**. I am a professor of a far wider academy, of which human nature is merely a part.'
2. 'What is going to happen here at **Midnight**? Why not tune into BBC3 at 11.45 tonight and find out.'
3. 'Oh, be not lily-livered now. This gold is not for weaklings.' 'I will not kill in **Cold Blood**.'
4. 'Wasn't there a plan once to build underground quarters for the government in the event of an atomic war?' 'Yes, back in the **Cold War** days.'
5. 'Halt. **Turn Left**. Move forward.'

6. '**Journey's End**, Doctor. I'm sorry. Your cremation will deprive me of our periodic encounters.'
7. 'It nearly beat me. Such a simple, brutal power. Just the power of **Tooth and Claw**.'
8. 'A fair **Rose** of England in this foreign land.'
9. 'There we were, the skin of a gnat's whisker from **The Big Bang**, and—' 'And nothing happened at all.'

10. 'A right old Fred Karno's Army, innit? Still, not to worry, me old son. Not **The End of the World**, is it? Want some more tea?'

11. 'You should be grateful to help me. We'll begin a **New Earth**, the centre of a new empire.'

12. 'It's a **Doomsday** weapon, mister, and rightly primed it could split that planet in half.'

13. 'What is it?' 'How would I know, but it certainly isn't **Closing Time** at Betty Murphy's pub.'

14. 'Oh, I'm right. Hercules 208 in Messier 13 is definitely on the **Blink**.'

15. 'Oh, Doctor, these things'll follow us to **The End of Time**. They'll never give up either.'

Titles Within Titles 2

Can you identify the stories in which these pre-1996 story titles (give or take a definite article) crop up in post-2005 dialogue?

1. 'Begin **The Invasion** of Manhattan. The population will be converted into Daleks.'
2. 'Let the Christmas **Inferno** commence.'
3. 'They say the gods of the **Underworld** are stirring.'
4. 'I find her and then what do I do? This isn't an alien invasion. They live here. This is their empire. This is kicking **The Romans** out of Rome.'
5. 'Help me, I'm being driven by a **Robot**!'

6. '**Three Doctors**?!' 'I can't tell you what I'm thinking right now.'
7. 'It's a **Battlefield** graveyard. My final battle.'
8. 'And that is why we are in a unique position today, my friend, to end this **Reign of Terror**. So – feeling like painting the church today?'
9. 'They tell legends of Mars. From long ago. Of a fine and noble race, who built an empire out of snow. **The Ice Warriors**.'
10. 'Skaro. The original **Planet of the Daleks**. Look at the state of it.'

11. 'Hush, now. I need some information from your data core. Everything **The Daleks** know about the Silence.'
12. 'Driver, be swift! **The Chase** is on!'
13. 'The Eye of Harmony. Exploding star in the act of becoming a black hole. Time Lord engineering. You rip the star from its orbit, suspend it in a permanent **State of Decay**.'
14. '**Survival** estimate projection, zero per cent.'
15. 'What about **The Rescue**, how long's it going to take?' 'About 60 minutes, that's all.'

Titles Within Titles 3

Can you identify the stories in which these Hartnell episode titles crop up in post-2005 dialogue?

1. '… Just going down to **The Lion**! Quick little snifter! Christmas drinks!'
2. 'Oh sweet Dolly Bailey. She sat out three bouts of **The Plague** in this place.'
3. 'Couldn't tell the difference between **The Escape** pod and the bathroom – we had to go back for her. Twice.'
4. 'Clarence DeMarco. Murderer, under **Sentence of Death**. He offered us this in exchange for his life.'
5. 'It's a ship. Dreadnought class. Front line of an **Invasion**.'

6. 'First of all you drug me, then you **Kidnap** me, and don't think I didn't feel your hands having a quick wander, you dirty old man.'
7. 'All right, he's a nutter. Off his head. Complete alien **Conspiracy** freak.'
8. 'We move to **The Final Phase**! Prepare the subjugation of Earth.'
9. 'Another friend of mine brought him back. I'm not sure all his brains made **The Return** trip.'

10. 'I came here when I was just a kid. Ninety years old. It was **The Centre** of a rift in time and space.'

11. '**Air Lock** sealed. Jettison escape pod.'
12. 'Right, You've been ordered to kill **The Survivors**, but why?'
13. 'Knocked off before I left – told 'em I had a family **Crisis**.'
14. '**The Death of Time**. The end of time. The end of us all. Oh, why couldn't you just die?'
15. 'I can't do it. I need both hearts!' 'All right. **Desperate Measures**.'

Problematic Production Codes

Between 1963 and 1989, every *Doctor Who* story had an alphabetical production code. Identify the code for each story given here. The resultant letters form an anagram of another story title. Rearrange the letters to identify that story! (NB 4A = AAAA etc.)

1. *The Chase, The Daleks, Galaxy 4, The Ice Warriors*
2. *The Power of the Daleks, Fury from the Deep, The Aztecs, An Unearthly Child, The Reign of Terror*
3. *The Daleks, The Edge of Destruction, The Time Monster, The Tenth Planet, The Evil of the Daleks*
4. *The Daleks, The Web Planet, Galaxy 4, The Massacre, The Romans, The Time Monster*
5. *The Web Planet, The Massacre, The Chase, The Reign of Terror, Mission to the Unknown, The Power of the Daleks*

6. *An Unearthly Child, The Edge of Destruction, The Rescue, The Romans, The Crusade, The Time Monster, The Chase*
7. *An Unearthly Child, The Power of the Daleks, The Moonbase, The Tomb of the Cybermen, The Dominators, The Dalek Invasion of Earth, The Chase, The Time Meddler, The Celestial Toymaker*
8. *An Unearthly Child, The Aztecs, The Reign of Terror, The Myth*

Makers, *The Web Planet, The Time Meddler, The Three Doctors, The Green Death, The Time Monster, The Power of the Daleks*

9. *The Ice Warriors, The Ice Warriors* (again), *The Robots of Death, The Highlanders, The Reign of Terror, An Unearthly Child, The Web Planet, The Sensorites, The Edge of Destruction, The Dalek Invasion of Earth*

10. *The Savages, The Invasion, Terror of the Autons, The Mutants, The Ice Warriors, The Sensorites, The Edge of Destruction, The Chase, The Time Meddler*

11. *The Reign of Terror, The Chase, An Unearthly Child, The Web Planet, The Time Meddler, The Dominators, The Smugglers, The Power of the Daleks, The Ice Warriors, The Tenth Planet*

12. *The Dominators, The Moonbase, Genesis of the Daleks, Fury from the Deep, The Ice Warriors, The Crusade, The Massacre, The Aztecs*

13. *The Savages, Inferno, The Abominable Snowmen, The Keys of Marinus, The Myth Makers, The Celestial Toymaker, The Chase, The Massacre, The Romans*

14. *The Ribos Operation, The Invisible Enemy, The Moonbase, Terror of the Autons, The Mutants, The Sensorites, The Rescue, The Time Meddler, The Dalek Invasion of Earth, The Romans*

15. *The Green Death, The Moonbase, Genesis of the Daleks, The Ice Warriors, The Tomb of the Cybermen, The War Machines, The Aztecs, The Edge of Destruction, The Celestial Toymaker, The Chase, The Web Planet*

Metamorphoses

Add extra letters to turn one *Doctor Who* term into another one! The new letters may go before, after or either side of the original word, while leaving it intact. Which two words are being described in each question?

1. Add two letters to a companion to turn her into one of her successors.
2. Add one letter to transfer an Australian into a Mongol.
3. Add one letter to transform a princess into a Silurian.
4. Add four letters to turn a companion into a companion's home town.
5. Add one letter to transform a monster into a masterful alias.

6. Add three letters to transform a peaceful race into a planet's ruler.
7. Add four letters to transform a planet containing duplicates into a clone race.
8. Add five letters to turn a mining representative into a race found underground.
9. Add three letters to mutate a mad scientist into a mutant.
10. Add four letters to transform a companion into a companion's supposed protector.

11. Add three letters to turn a companion invisible.
12. Add six letters to turn a monster that can't speak into one that hates noise.
13. Add six letters to transform a companion into a monster that once transformed into a companion.
14. Add six letters to transform a villain seeking power into pure energy.
15. Add three letters to turn a pirate planet into a shapeshifter.

And Now on BBC One…

Unanswerable Questions

There are undoubtedly many people who've managed to get the last 2,985 questions right. So, just for fun, here are fifteen questions that no one can get right – at least, with reference to the television series only – but equally, no one can get wrong. Dust off your fan ingenuity and try these unanswerable (at the time of writing) questions…

1. If Susan's the Doctor's granddaughter, what happened to her mum and dad? (Also: can she regenerate? Are all Gallifreyans Time Lords? Time Lords: born or made? And is her real name Susan or something more like Susandvoratrelundar?)
2. Who were those faces in *The Brain of Morbius*? (Or to put it another way: How far, Doctor? How long have you lived?) (And: is 'the First Doctor' the first Doctor?)
3. What is the Doctor's name?
4. How did Ace leave the Doctor?
5. How did the Doctor meet Mel?
6. Who was 'The Waking Ally'?
7. What are the real names for the Ice Warrior, Silurian and Sea Devil races (yes, they've started using those names themselves now, but that's just bowing to public pressure,

isn't it)?

8. Did Susan really make up the name TARDIS? (And: Dimension or Dimensions?)
9. Is Dodo descended from Anne Chaplet? (And let's not go near 'was Steven Dodo's great great etc. grandfather?')
10. Voord: men in rubber suits, or monsters who look like men in rubber suits? (And: Voord or Voords?)
11. What was that Dalek doing in the Thames?
12. What happened in Captain Jack's missing two years?
13. How old is the Doctor?
14. Was Sarah Jane really from 1980, or was she just confused?

And always remember, if there's something in *Doctor Who* that doesn't seem to make sense – following *The Name of the Doctor*, the explanation is probably 'Clara'. You need never be stumped for an answer again…

The End

1. The introduction to this book promised there would be at least one question relating to every single televised *Doctor Who* story. What is the only story that has not had a reference made to either its name or content anywhere in the previous 2,999 questions?

The Answers

Pre-Titles Sequence

Page 23 – The Doctors
1. David Tennant
2. Tom Baker
3. Jon Pertwee
4. Matt Smith
5. Peter Capaldi
6. Peter Davison
7. Patrick Troughton
8. Colin Baker
9. William Hartnell
10. Sylvester McCoy
11. Christopher Eccleston
12. Paul McGann
13. John Hurt
14. Michael Jayston
15. Richard Hurndall

Page 24 – The Companions 1
1. Catherine Tate
2. Karen Gillan
3. Nicholas Courtney

4. Frazer Hines
5. Noel Clarke
6. William Russell
7. Maureen O'Brien
8. Katy Manning
9. Nicola Bryant
10. Wendy Padbury
11. Jean Marsh
12. Sarah Sutton
13. Michael Craze
14. Daphne Ashbrook
15. John Levene

Page 25 – The Companions 2
1. Billie Piper
2. Alex Kingston
3. Jenna (formerly Jenna-Louise) Coleman
4. Bernard Cribbins
5. Elisabeth Sladen
6. Carole Ann Ford
7. Deborah Watling
8. Mary Tamm
9. Bonnie Langford
10. Caroline John
11. Peter Purves
12. Ian Marter
13. Adrienne Hill
14. Matthew Waterhouse

15. Mark Strickson

Page 26 – The Companions 3
1. Louise Jameson
2. Freema Agyeman
3. John Barrowman
4. Arthur Darvill
5. Sophie Aldred
6. John Leeson
7. Lalla Ward
8. Janet Fielding
9. Jacqueline Hill
10. Anneke Wills
11. Jackie Lane
12. Gerald Flood
13. Richard Franklin
14. Bruno Langley
15. Yee Jee Tso

Page 27 – Talkin' About Regeneration
1. *The Tenth Planet*
2. *The War Games*
3. *Planet of the Spiders*
4. *Logopolis*
5. *The Caves of Androzani*
6. *Time and the Rani*
7. *The Parting of the Ways*

8. *The End of Time, Part Two*
9. *The Time of the Doctor*
10. *Doctor Who* (TV movie)
11. *The Day of the Doctor*
12. *The Night of the Doctor*
13. *Planet of the Spiders*
14. Romana and River Song
15. According to the Master, somewhere between the Doctor's twelfth and final incarnations

Page 28 – Hello, Goodbye 1

1. Susan
2. Martha
3. Nyssa
4. Jo
5. Jamie
6. Peri
7. Harry
8. Turlough
9. Romana 1
10. Tegan
11. Ben and Polly
12. K-9 Mark I
13. Steven
14. Katarina
15. Kamelion

Page 29 – Hello, Goodbye 2

1. Rose
2. Adric
3. Donna
4. Ace
5. Ian and Barbara
6. Sarah Jane
7. Liz
8. Leela
9. Romana 2
10. Vicki
11. Mel
12. Adam
13. Sara Kingdom
14. Dodo
15. Zoe

Page 30 – Personal Possessions 1

1. The Fourth Doctor
2. The Fifth Doctor
3. The Seventh Doctor
4. The Sixth Doctor
5. The Eleventh Doctor
6. The Ninth Doctor
7. The Fourth Doctor
8. The Eleventh Doctor
9. The Third Doctor
10. The Seventh Doctor

11. The Second Doctor
12. The First Doctor
13. The Fifth Doctor
14. The Eighth Doctor
15. The Tenth Doctor

Page 31 – Personal Possessions 2

1. Adric
2. Clara
3. Jamie
4. Ace
5. Amy
6. Leela
7. Rory
8. Captain Jack
9. Zoe
10. K-9
11. The Brigadier
12. Grace
13. Nyssa
14. Sarah Jane
15. Steven

Page 32 – Name That Story 1

1. *Black Orchid*
2. *Hide*
3. *Planet of Giants*

4. *Marco Polo*
5. *Closing Time*
6. *Planet of the Spiders*
7. *State of Decay*
8. *Asylum of the Daleks*
9. *The Reign of Terror*
10. *The Unquiet Dead*
11. *The Crimson Horror*
12. *The Horns of Nimon*
13. *The Angels Take Manhattan*
14. *The Hungry Earth*
15. *Tooth and Claw*

Page 33 – Name That Story 2

1. *Carnival of Monsters*
2. *Cold Blood*
3. *Human Nature*
4. *Day of the Moon*
5. *Warriors' Gate*
6. *City of Death*
7. *Nightmare in Silver*
8. *Dinosaurs on a Spaceship*
9. *The Impossible Planet*
10. *Daleks in Manhattan*
11. *The Underwater Menace*
12. *The End of Time*
13. *The Unicorn and the Wasp*
14. *Terror of the Autons*

15. *The Power of Three*

Page 34 – Title Hunt 1
1. *Logopolis*
2. *Inferno*
3. *Meglos*
4. *The Ark*
5. *Ghost Light*
6. *Mawdryn Undead*
7. *Mission to the Unknown*
8. *Fury from the Deep*
9. *Planet of the Spiders*
10. *The Greatest Show in the Galaxy*
11. *The Two Doctors*
12. *The Invisible Enemy*
13. *The Ribos Operation*
14. *The Evil of the Daleks*
15. *The Monster of Peladon*

Page 35 – Title Hunt 2
1. *Utopia*
2. *New Earth*
3. *Night Terrors*
4. *Closing Time*
5. *A Christmas Carol*
6. *Journey to the Centre of the TARDIS*
7. *Evolution of the Daleks*

8. *The Doctor's Daughter*
9. *Partners in Crime*
10. *The Next Doctor*
11. *The Pandorica Opens*
12. *Aliens of London*
13. *Army of Ghosts*
14. *The Poison Sky*
15. *Silence in the Library*

Page 36 – Births and Birthdays

1. *The Power of the Daleks*
2. *Spearhead from Space*
3. *Robot*
4. *Castrovalva*
5. *The Twin Dilemma*
6. *Time and the Rani*
7. *Rose*
8. *The Christmas Invasion*
9. *The Eleventh Hour*
10. *The Three Doctors*
11. *The Five Doctors*
12. *Silver Nemesis*
13. *Dimensions in Time*
14. *The Day of the Doctor*
15. *The Stones of Blood*

Opening Titles

Page 39 – Initially – A

1. Adipose
2. Alzarius
3. Andromeda
4. Adrasta
5. Aggedor
6. Arthur
7. Atraxi
8. Athelstan
9. Atropine
10. Aris
11. Amdo
12. Alison
13. Azure
14. Argonite
15. Arianna

Page 41 – Initially – B

1. Bok
2. Borusa
3. Bessie
4. Bennett

5. Banto
6. Biodamper
7. The *Buccaneer*
8. BOSS
9. Bandrils
10. Blackbeard
11. Boscawen
12. The *Byzantium*
13. Bliss
14. Buffalo
15. Bostock

Page 42 – Initially – C

1. Craig
2. Cloister
3. Cryons
4. The CyberKing
5. Chip
6. Cyril
7. Cailleach
8. Culloden
9. Cherub
10. Constantine
11. The Corsair
12. The Caber
13. Cheen
14. Crichton
15. Caligari

Episode One
The Doctor and Co

Page 47 – The First Doctor

1. Dr Foreman
2. She looks like his 'grandchild, Susan'
3. The Reign of Terror (the French Revolution)
4. The Daleks
5. The Abbot of Amboise
6. Fifty
7. Kublai Khan
8. The Doctor in bathing suit and hat
9. Alcohol
10. Dido
11. Esto
12. Beau Brummell
13. The Traveller from Beyond Time
14. Keycodes of all the machines in the TARDIS and notes of everywhere they've been to
15. *The Vampires of Venice*

Page 49 – The Second Doctor

1. The First Doctor's ring
2. Doctor von Wer

3. Doctor-Gond
4. Brigadier Lethbridge-Stewart
5. Jamie
6. The Earth Examiner
7. The First World War
8. His favourite umbrella
9. Dulkis
10. That he repeatedly broke their most important law of non-interference in the affairs of other planets
11. Candle wax and marbles
12. He says he is the Doctor's assistant
13. They think he is Salamander
14. He uses the Rough and Tumble machine
15. That he teaches the Doctor to play the bagpipes

Page 51 – The Third Doctor

1. Venusian
2. The Moon
3. Fire
4. In his shoe
5. Harry Houdini
6. A galactic yoyo
7. A milkman (Jones's Da) and a cleaning lady (Doris)
8. Several thousand years
9. Irongron
10. Draughts
11. Nine, including *The Five Doctors*
12. Credentials

13. A Time Flow Analogue
14. Greed (for knowledge and information)
15. Dr Beavis

Page 53 – The Fourth Doctor

1. The Doctor's scarf
2. Theta Sigma
3. Prydonian
4. So he can invoke Article 17 and be guaranteed liberty
5. A captain in Cleopatra's bodyguard
6. Crossed computers
7. Over the teeth and down the throat
8. 51 per cent
9. When replacing a robot brain, always make sure the arrow A is pointing to the front
10. Sarah Jane
11. The Intergalactic Floral Society
12. The Droge of Gabrielides
13. 749
14. 759
15. 523 years

Page 55 – The Fifth Doctor

1. Omega
2. Adric's badge for Mathematical Excellence
3. The Harp of Rassilon
4. Adric

5. Sonic screwdriver
6. Harlequin
7. Effete
8. It turns purple at the presence of certain gases in the praxis range of the spectrum to which he is allergic
9. It would use up his remaining regenerations
10. A zero cabinet
11. To assassinate the High Council
12. He's not ready for it
13. Guildford
14. Destroy the signal box that summons him
15. Sir John Sudbury (Department C19)

Page 57 – The Sixth Doctor

1. Azmael
2. Commodore 'Tonker' Travers
3. Repairing the TARDIS's Chameleon Circuit
4. Vegetarianism
5. Genocide
6. He was deposed due to wilfully neglecting the responsibility of the great office
7. Yellow (with stars)
8. The Inquisitor
9. Stoning
10. Arthur Stengos
11. Titan III
12. Kew Gardens
13. Herbert (H.G. Wells)

14. A warlord of Thordon
15. 'Ancient Life on Ravalox'

Page 59 – The Seventh Doctor

1. Burnt toast
2. Straight blowing
3. Melt the snowman
4. Merlin
5. Bessie
6. Lady Peinforte
7. The names of his companions
8. His umbrella
9. Three gunshot wounds
10. A week's holiday in Disneyland, 1959
11. 953
12. Blue on one side and red on the other
13. A question mark on a black seal
14. 900
15. 1928 hibiscus blossom

Page 61 – The Eighth Doctor

1. Dr Bowman
2. His soul
3. A Wild Bill Hickok outfit
4. Anaesthetic
5. Brian's
6. A fire hose

7. In a secret cubbyhole above the 'P' in Police Box
8. *Frankenstein*
9. 20lb
10. Madame Curie
11. At the opera
12. The second
13. A Beryllium chip
14. 250 million light years
15. Ten minutes

Paeg 63 – The Ninth Doctor

1. Clive's
2. A champagne cork
3. Air from his lungs
4. Ricky
5. Being slapped by someone's mother
6. Suki
7. Dr John Smith, Ministry of Asteroids
8. Reattaches barbed wire
9. The *Western Mail*
10. Mr Spock
11. The Oncoming Storm
12. Five billion
13. The Heathen
14. Kyoto in 1336
15. Burnt fingers

Paeg 65 – The Tenth Doctor

1. His right hand
2. 'I don't want to go.'
3. His tie
4. Chameleon Arch
5. Metacrisis
6. Ood Sigma
7. The smell of tea
8. Sir Doctor of TARDIS
9. Physics
10. The banana daiquiri
11. Elton Pope
12. Sunday
13. Break his heart
14. The King of Belgium
15. The Time Lord Victorious

Page 67 – The Eleventh Doctor

1. The Caretaker
2. Sexy
3. Monster
4. A Jammie Dodger biscuit
5. A Cyberman's head
6. Don't wander off
7. The Doctor lies
8. Nefertiti and Riddell
9. Sherlock Holmes
10. Clara

11. The crack in the universe
12. Apples
13. The Soothsayer
14. A chicken
15. He headbutts him

Page 69 – Don't Give up the Day Job

1. Amy
2. Martha
3. Tegan
4. Sarah Jane
5. Jamie
6. Ben
7. Sara Kingdom
8. Barbara
9. Ian
10. Harry
11. Peri
12. Mel
13. Rory
14. Steven
15. Zoe

Page 70 – What's in a Name?

1. Dorothy
2. Dorothea
3. Foreman

4. Vislor
5. Astrid
6. Perpugillium
7. Jo Grant
8. The Face of Boe
9. Robert
10. Melody Pond
11. Jessica
12. John
13. Arthur
14. Prentice
15. Marion

Page 71 – Relative Dimensions

1. Jo Grant
2. Donna Noble
3. Sarah Jane Smith
4. Sara Kingdom
5. Victoria Waterfield
6. Rose Tyler
7. Peri Brown
8. Leela
9. Lady Christina de Souza
10. Ace
11. Adelaide Brooke
12. Vicki
13. Dodo Chaplet
14. Tegan

15. Mickey Smith

Page 72 – Companions – The First Doctor
1. High Priest Yetaxa
2. High Priestess Cassandra
3. Anne Chaplet
4. Vicki
5. Whipsnade
6. Astra
7. Black with thin emerald green stripes on it
8. Nero
9. About two years
10. Five months
11. Mike Yates
12. Kembel and Paris
13. Eprin
14. Leon Colbert
15. HMS *Teazer*

Page 74 – Companions – The Second Doctor
1. Duchess
2. The Tenth Doctor
3. His travelling with the Doctor makes him unique
4. Jamie and Zoe
5. Daleks
6. Donald Macrimmon
7. Chelsea, 1966

8. Michelle Leuppi
9. Kaiser Pudding
10. The Phantom Piper
11. The Parapsychology Library
12. A disposable transistor radio
13. A brewery
14. Jamie and Victoria
15. Benzene, ether, alcohol, acetone and epoxy-propane

Page 76 – Companions – The Third Doctor

1. Her aunt, Lavinia Smith
2. The blue Metebelis crystal
3. Section Leader
4. Princess Josephine of TARDIS
5. Latep
6. Miss Hawthorne
7. Liz Shaw and Mike Yates
8. A man from the Ministry
9. Ace
10. Uxarieus
11. Official status as a United Nations Priority One Research Complex for the Wholeweal Community
12. *Metropolitan*
13. A watch
14. Jupiter
15. 23

Page 78 – Companions – The Fourth Doctor

1. E-Space
2. Ginger beer
3. 1980
4. Janis thorns
5. The flash of light from the destruction of a Rutan ship
6. Buy himself out of the Navy, buy a quiet little practice in the country and have a solid gold stethoscope
7. Tennis
8. The Bureau of Ancient Records
9. Laryngitis
10. Varsh's belt
11. Four
12. Intercity train
13. The arms
14. 125
15. Floating down the Amazon in a hatbox

Page 80 – Companions – The Fifth Doctor

1. Ice cream
2. A mouth on legs
3. Her cousin, Colin Frazer
4. Ann Talbot
5. The Black Guardian
6. Xeriphas
7. Misos Triangle
8. He's wearing his badge which had been destroyed
9. The TARDIS's hat stand

10. The walk's not quite right – and then there's the accent
11. A Delta Wave Augmenter
12. Navigator
13. 778
14. Morocco
15. Junior Ensign Commander

Page 82 – Companions – The Sixth Doctor

1. A bird
2. Luke Ward, who's been turned into a tree
3. Carrot juice
4. Perpugillium of the Brown
5. Pease Pottage
6. She's looking for suitable accommodation for American students
7. Amalgamation with a Morlox before becoming his bride and repopulating Karfel
8. The DJ's accent and presentation style
9. An elephant
10. Jamie
11. Tegan, Zoe, Susan, Jamie
12. Herbabaculum vitae – the Staff of Life
13. Being fed into the pulveriser
14. Valerian
15. The Raak

Page 84 – Companions – The Seventh Doctor

1. Waitress
2. Karra
3. Doughnut
4. Professor
5. A baseball bat
6. A shawl and a toasting fork
7. Discretion
8. 13
9. C.P. Snow
10. His Red Star badge
11. Exotic alien swords
12. Charlton Athletic
13. The Fourth Doctor's scarf
14. Mrs Parkinson the art teacher
15. 17 Old Terrace, Streatham

Page 85 – Companions – The Eighth Doctor

1. Amazing Grace
2. *Madame Butterfly*
3. Afraid of dying
4. The Asian Child
5. Cardiology
6. Black
7. The Eye of Harmony
8. He breaks his neck
9. John Smith
10. Two bags of gold dust

11. A million bucks
12. The radio on his motorbike
13. The wrist
14. Next Christmas
15. Walker General

Page 86 – Companions – the Ninth Doctor

1. Her passport
2. *The Weakest Link*
3. Chips
4. His car
5. Union Jack
6. Finch's the butcher's
7. Hullabaloo
8. The Vomit-O-Matic
9. A Time Agent
10. Two and a half
11. 'Moonlight Serenade'
12. Defrabicator and Compact Laser Deluxe
13. He logged into the Pentagon defence system
14. Takes her for a picnic in the country
15. Shareen

Page 88 – Companions – The Tenth Doctor

1. Mickey Smith
2. Royal Hope Hospital
3. Dinner lady

4. Chiswick
5. Bad Wolf
6. The Vinvocci
7. Freedonia
8. Miss Evangelista
9. The Children of Time
10. Diamond earrings
11. 42
12. Astrid Peth
13. Lee McAvoy
14. Frederic
15. 21 November 2059

Page 89 – Companions – The Eleventh Doctor

1. Twelve years
2. A ponytail
3. She gives him her remaining regenerations
4. Rory
5. The Last Centurion
6. Petrichor
7. She couldn't have children
8. Angie and Artie Maitland
9. Ellie
10. Porridge (aka Emperor Ludens Nimrod Kendrick, called Longstaff the forty first, the Defender of Humanity, Imperator of known space)
11. 'Please don't change.'
12. Budgen's

13. E-type Jaguar
14. 'Raggedy man. Good night.'
15. 3 April 1938

Page 91 – Could've Been, Should've Been

1. Samantha Briggs
2. Jackson Lake
3. Ray
4. Madame de Pompadour
5. Duggan
6. Herbert (H.G. Wells)
7. The Gravis
8. Bret Vyon
9. Anne Chaplet
10. Will Chandler
11. Lynda Moss
12. Rita
13. Penny Carter
14. Jenny, in *The Dalek Invasion of Earth*
15. Sir Colin Thackery

Page 93 – The Tylers

1. Mickey
2. 'Doctor'
3. Fruit (apple and satsuma)
4. Granddad Prentice
5. Rose

6. Vitex health drinks
7. Mrs Croot
8. Her washing machine
9. Andrea Suzette
10. Sarah Jane Smith
11. 7 November 1987
12. 48 Bucknall House
13. His axle broke
14. Jordan Road
15. Cliff Richard movies

Page 95 – The Joneses

1. Annalise
2. Shoot the Master
3. Harold Saxon
4. Soap
5. Torchwood One, Canary Wharf
6. The Cybermen
7. That she and Clive are back together
8. Leo's 21st birthday party
9. Head of the PR Department
10. Keisha
11. Brighton
12. The islands of Japan burning
13. Who had the most Number Ones, Elvis or the Beatles?
14. The Bell Tower
15. Project Indigo

Page 97 – The Nobles

1. Newspaper vendor
2. Geoffrey
3. Donna Temple-Noble
4. Their computer has no webcam
5. A paint gun
6. Private
7. He had Spanish flu
8. She breaks the windscreen with an axe
9. The Silver Cloak
10. Astronomy
11. Veni, vedi, vici
12. Palestine
13. Took a bus to Strathclyde
14. Suzette
15. In a bin on Brook Street

Page 98 – The Ponds

1. She carved faces onto them
2. Aunt Sharon
3. A stepladder
4. The National Museum
5. Augustus
6. 26 June 2010
7. Tabetha
8. A trowel
9. She remembers them
10. Thailand

11. The paper shop and golf
12. Henry VIII
13. 361
14. Siluria
15. He thinks he may have been using the same joke book as the Best Man

Page 100 – The Many Lives of Clara Oswald

1. The Impossible Girl
2. Soufflé Girl
3. Save the Doctor
4. 'Run you clever boy. And remember me.'
5. Driving Bessie
6. Svartos
7. Miss Montague
8. Gallifrey
9. In the Matrix
10. The navigation system
11. English
12. Brian Robson
13. Digby and Francesca
14. Starship *Alaska*
15. 23 November 1866

Page 102 – The Paternoster Gang

1. Parker
2. Nurse

3. Strax
4. Thomas Thomas
5. She vanishes
6. A lizard woman from the Dawn of Time
7. 13 Paternoster Row, London
8. Lock the doors
9. Stop their hearts
10. Mr Thursday
11. Clarence deMarco
12. In the London Underground
13. Dying in combat
14. Nearly 12
15. Automated laser monkeys

Page 104 – Companion Departures – 1960s

1. David Campbell
2. Troilus
3. The Elders and the Savages
4. The Time Destructor
5. Ben and Polly
6. Victoria
7. A Redcoat shoots at him
8. 1965
9. 20 July 1966
10. The Harrises
11. Tanya Lernov
12. 'Don't go blundering into too much trouble, will you?'
13. One of the daughters of the gods

14. A TARDIS key
15. White City underground station

Page 106 – Companion Departures – the 1970s

1. Cambridge
2. Cardiff
3. K-9 MII
4. The upper reaches of the Amazon
5. Hillview Road, South Croydon
6. 'Twin'
7. 'Daddy Wouldn't Buy Me a Bow-wow'
8. The TARDIS
9. The Tharils
10. The Metebelis blue crystal
11. A knife
12. Benton
13. A pelargonium (commonly known as a geranium)
14. 'You were the noblest Romana of them all.'
15. 'I feel fine.'

Page 108 – Companion Departures – the 1980s

1. Peri
2. Heathrow Airport
3. Yrcanos
4. Aunt Vanessa
5. Hydromel
6. Crozier

7. The Master's Tissue Compression Eliminator
8. Tegan's
9. Indestructible
10. Three
11. Terradon
12. Trion
13. Put it in a bottle and throw it into space
14. *Nosferatu II*
15. Peri

Page 110 – Companion Departures – 2005 onwards

1. She will burn up
2. Amy
3. Pete Tyler
4. Her mobile phone
5. A gravestone with his name on it
6. Because he thinks it will hurt him too much
7. Dalek Caan
8. A magnaclamp
9. Dr Thomas Milligan
10. 87
11. New York will be ripped apart
12. 'Raggedy man, goodbye.'
13. Because it is hard for her to leave when the Doctor hasn't said goodbye
14. A supernova
15. Charles II and Henry VIII

Closing Credits

Page 115 – Initially – D

1. Davros
2. Drums
3. Drahvins
4. Deadlock
5. Dulkis
6. Dill
7. Dragon
8. Devesham
9. Doomsday
10. Dynatrope
11. Dancer
12. Dupont
13. Diplos
14. Daisy
15. Dunbar

Page 116 – Initially – E

1. Eyepatch
2. Ember
3. Editor
4. Eternity

5. Expelliarmus
6. Ergon
7. Erato
8. Exxilon
9. Eldrad
10. Eureka
11. Eldane
12. Ephemerals
13. Eleanor
14. Eternal
15. Eden

Page 118 – Initially – F

1. Fang
2. Firestone
3. Fire
4. Fifi
5. Fendahleen
6. Fariah
7. Futurekind
8. Functionaries
9. Fenric
10. The *Fancy*
11. Flutterwing
12. Florana
13. Fred
14. Fizzade
15. Flora

Opening Titles (2)

Page 121 – Initially – G

1. Gadget
2. Game
3. Gelth
4. Gravitron
5. Girl
6. Gastropods
7. Galleia
8. Gavrok
9. Gulliver
10. Gibbis
11. Grendel
12. Gemini
13. Gatherer
14. Guiliano
15. Gern

Page 122 – Initially – H

1. Hal
2. Hartman
3. Henrik's
4. House

5. Halley's
6. Heretic
7. Hyperspace
8. Hame
9. Handbag
10. Hieronymous
11. Heliotrope
12. Hoob
13. Hoix
14. Harkaway
15. Horner

Page 124 – Initially – I

1. Idris
2. Ian
3. Immortality
4. Isolus
5. Ironsides
6. Irongron
7. India
8. Iceworld
9. Isop
10. Infostamp
11. Ixta
12. Icthar
13. Ioniser
14. Isabella
15. Ibbotson

Episode Two
Adventures in Time and Space

Page 127 – Time Travel – Past

1. *The Time Meddler*   1066
2. *The Romans*   64
3. *The Visitation*   1666
4. *The Empty Child*   1941
5. *The Reign of Terror*   1794
6. *The King's Demons*   1215
7. *Black Orchid*   1925
8. *Delta and the Bannermen*   1959
9. *Marco Polo*   1289
10. *The Massacre*   1572
11. *Pyramids of Mars*   1911
12. *The Next Doctor*   1851
13. *Ghost Light*   1883
14. *The Gunfighters*   1881
15. *The Unquiet Dead*   1869

Page 128 – Time Travel – Present (or is it)?

1. *Mawdryn Undead* (earlier time zone)   1977
2. *Remembrance of the Daleks*   1963
3. *Doctor Who* (TV movie)   1999

4.	Rose	2005
5.	Fear Her	2012
6.	Aliens of London	2006
7.	Logopolis	1981
8.	City of Death	1979
9.	Silver Nemesis	1988
10.	The Awakening	1984
11.	The Faceless Ones	1966
12.	The Tenth Planet	1986
13.	Hide	1974
14.	Father's Day	1987
15.	Cold War	1983

Page 129 – Time Travel – Future

1.	The Daleks' Master Plan	4000
2.	The Invisible Enemy	5000
3.	The End of the World	5,000,000,000
4.	New Earth	5,000,000,023
5.	Gridlock	5,000,000,053
6.	The Moonbase	2070
7.	Planet of Evil	37,166
8.	The Enemy of the World	2018
9.	Warriors of the Deep	2084
10.	Colony in Space	2472
11.	Earthshock	2526
12.	Dinosaurs on a Spaceship	2367
13.	Terror of the Vervoids	2986
14.	The Leisure Hive	2290

15. *Nightmare of Eden*   2116

Page 130 – Name-Dropping

1. The Eleventh Doctor
2. The Tenth Doctor
3. The Eighth Doctor
4. The First Doctor
5. The First Doctor
6. The Fourth Doctor
7. The Third Doctor
8. The Fourth Doctor
9. The Fourth Doctor
10. The Eleventh Doctor
11. The First Doctor
12. The Seventh Doctor
13. The Fourth Doctor
14. The First Doctor
15. The Tenth Doctor

Page 131 – Planet-Hopping

1. Mondas
2. Telos
3. Midnight
4. Traken
5. Deva Loka
6. Segonax
7. Atrios and Zeos

8. Clom
9. San Helios
10. Aneth
11. Barcelona
12. Delphon
13. Woman Wept
14. Alfava Metraxis
15. Castor 36

Page 133 – Could You Say That Again?

1. Song River
2. Melkur
3. Hello Sweetie
4. Sanctuary Base 6
5. Bad Wolf
6. German
7. (a) Magister (b) Thascales
8. 'Silence must fall'
9. Doctor
10. Doktor von Wer
11. Bad Wolf Bay
12. Bitter Pill
13. Vashta Nerada
14. Rev Wainwright
15. Mickey Smith

Page 135 – The Real World

1. *The Sea Devils*
2. *The Sound of Drums*
3. *Army of Ghosts*
4. *Aliens of London*
5. *The Sound of Drums*
6. *The Eleventh Hour*
7. *Silver Nemesis*
8. *The Power of Three*
9. *The Stolen Earth*
10. *Aliens of London | World War Three*
11. *The Poison Sky*
12. *The Power of Three*
13. *The War Machines*
14. *The Day of the Daleks*
15. *Silence in the Library*

Page 136 – Inspector Gadget

1. *Human Nature*
2. *Remembrance of the Daleks*
3. *Fury from the Deep*
4. *The Power of the Daleks*
5. *The Armageddon Factor*
6. *The Daleks*
7. *The Sound of Drums*
8. *Dragonfire*
9. *The End of the World*
10. *The Daleks*

11. *Doctor Who and the Silurians*
12. *Logopolis*
13. *The Three Doctors* (first time the Doctor offers one to anyone)
14. *Revenge of the Cybermen*
15. *The Time of Angels*

Page 137 – Never Seen Again
1. Blink
2. *Let's Kill Hitler*
3. *The Moonbase*
4. *The Impossible Astronaut*
5. *The Chase* (it's obtained in *The Space Museum* but not seen until the next story)
6. *The Ambassadors of Death*
7. *The Time Monster*
8. *The Daemons*
9. *Planet of the Daleks*
10. *The Android Invasion*
11. *The Daleks' Master Plan*
12. *The Web Planet*
13. *State of Decay*
14. *The Keeper of Traken*
15. *Timelash*

Page 138 – I Cross the Void Beyond the Mind…
1. Time Scoop
2. Ian and Barbara

3. Time ring
4. Ace
5. Martha
6. Star Whales
7. The Master
8. Static
9. T-Mat (short for Travel-Mat)
10. Travel dials
11. Vortex Manipulator
12. The Timelash
13. Mice
14. Tharils
15. The Brothers Hop Pyleen

Page 140 – Writerly Riddles 1 – Shakespeare

1. *The Chase*
2. Vicki (Cressida)
3. *The Da Vinci Code*
4. *Love's Labour's Lost*
5. Martha
6. Oscar Botcherby
7. Sycorax
8. Grief from the loss of his son
9. *Hamlet*
10. The psychic paper appears blank to him
11. (b) 'Once more unto the breach'
12. *Planet of Evil*
13. *The Masque of Mandragora*

14. Falstaff in love
15. The Sixth Doctor

Page 142 – Writerly Riddles 2 – Agatha Christie
1. *Murder on the Orient Express*
2. Minnie Hooper
3. Mark Gatiss
4. Donna
5. Once
6. *The Murder of Roger Ackroyd*
7. *Last of the Time Lords*
8. (a) *Hickory Dickory Dock*
9. She'd discovered her husband was having an affair
10. *Death in the Clouds*
11. A scrap of paper with the word 'maiden' written on it
12. 'Belgians make such lovely buns.'
13. Colin Baker
14. *The Smugglers*
15. 1926

Page 144 – Writerly Riddles 3 – Charles Dickens
1. Mrs Peace
2. 24 December 1869
3. *A Christmas Carol*
4. For ever
5. Charlie
6. 'The Signalman'

7. The American bit of *Martin Chuzzlewit*
8. The death of Little Nell
9. *Hard Times*
10. Sidney Carton
11. 'The Mystery of Edwin Drood and the Blue Elementals'
12. Taliesin Lodge
13. Sian Williams and Bill Turnbull
14. Peter Capaldi
15. Paul McGann

Page 146 – True or False 1 – Metals and Minerals

1. True
2. False
3. True
4. True
5. False
6. False
7. True
8. True
9. False
10. True (and real!)
11. False
12. True
13. False
14. True
15. True

Page 147 – True or False 2 – TARDIS Bits

1. False
2. True
3. False
4. False
5. True
6. True
7. True
8. True
9. False
10. False
11. True
12. False
13. False
14. True
15. True

Page 148 – True or False 3 – Planets

1. True
2. True
3. False
4. False
5. True
6. False
7. True
8. False
9. True
10. True

11. True
12. True
13. False
14. True
15. False

Page 149 – True or False 4 – UNIT personnel

1. True
2. True
3. True
4. False
5. False
6. True
7. True
8. False
9. False
10. False
11. False
12. True
13. True
14. True
15. True

Page 150 – Time Lord Biology

1. Six minutes
2. Respiratory bypass system
3. How to stop her hearts

4. G-Force
5. The Ninth Doctor
6. *Spearhead from Space*
7. *The Edge of Destruction*
8. He shakes it into his left shoe
9. Oxygen
10. Once every ten seconds
11. Ten beats a minute
12. 170
13. Symbiotic nuclei
14. The platelet stickiness
15. 300

Page 152 – Family and Early Life

1. Susan
2. Human
3. *The Doctor's Daughter*
4. The Master
5. Eight
6. He ran away
7. *Fear Her*
8. *The Tomb of the Cybermen*
9. Thermodynamics
10. K'Anpo Rimpoche
11. 'The Doctor's first stars'
12. Kathleen Dudman
13. 'No, not any more.'
14. 'You've been watching too much TV.'

15. A meteor storm

Page 154 – Fruit 'n' veg

1. Celery
2. Peach
3. Sir Walter Raleigh
4. Apple
5. Orange
6. Carrot
7. Bananas
8. Satsuma
9. Gherkins
10. Tomatoes
11. Pineapple
12. Pomegranate
13. Vivien Fay
14. Penley
15. Cabbage

Page 156 – Bookworms

1. Pandora's Box
2. River Song
3. *The Day of the Doctor*
4. The Library
5. The French Revolution
6. *The Tale of Peter Rabbit*
7. *Summer Falls* by Amelia Williams

8. *The Chase*
9. *Black Orchid*
10. *'Amelia's Last Farewell'*
11. Verity Newman
12. *Teach Yourself Tibetan*
13. *Little Women*
14. *Destiny of the Daleks*
15. *Juggling for the Complete Klutz*

Page 158 – Music to my Ears

1. Love & Monsters
2. *Last of the Time Lords*
3. *The Power of Three*
4. *The Chase*
5. *The End of the World*
6. *Father's Day*
7. *Rise of the Cybermen*
8. *Aliens of London*
9. *The Rings of Akhaten*
10. *Partners in Crime*
11. *Doctor Who* (TV movie)
12. *The Invasion*
13. *The Evil of the Daleks*
14. *Spearhead from Space*
15. *Revelation of the Daleks*

Page 159 – UNIT Good Guys

1. Sgt Osgood
2. Dr Malcolm Taylor
3. Captain Hawkins
4. Captain Jimmy Turner
5. Corporal Bell
6. Captain Munro
7. Zbrigniev
8. Mr Campbell
9. Sgt Henderson
10. Ross Jenkins
11. Colonel Mace
12. McGillop
13. Jenkins
14. Flight Lieutenant Lavel
15. Major Blake

Page 161 – Christmas Conundrums 1

1. 'Jingle Bells'
2. The Queen's speech
3. (a) 'My Angel Put The Devil In Me'
4. The great god Santa
5. Abigail
6. 1965
7. To spend Christmas with his family and make amends to them
8. The Racnoss spaceship
9. He did

10. *Fighting the Future* by Joshua Naismith
11. Naples
12. Pink
13. Red
14. Christmas tree bauble bombs
15. The Traveller's Halt

Page 163 – Christmas Conundrums 2

1. His regeneration energy
2. A Satsuma
3. (b) 24 December
4. Astrid
5. 'Incidentally, a happy Christmas to all of you at home'
6. The Doctor coming back
7. 'Good King Wenceslas'
8. 'Pond'
9. The country of Turkey
10. The Queen and Wilf
11. Dad, Gran and Linda
12. 'God Rest You Merry Gentlemen'
13. The Crystal Feast
14. Jeff
15. 'Good King Wenceslas'

Page 165 – Till Death Us Do Part

1. A vase
2. Marilyn Monroe

3. King Peladon
4. He makes and shares a drink of cocoa with her
5. The Tenth Doctor
6. The TARDIS
7. Saphadin
8. She will become a widow
9. Geoffrey Noble
10. Dance
11. Minnie Hooper
12. The Doctor's bow tie
13. St Mary's Church, Chiswick
14. Three
15. He drinks a potion of quicksilver and sulphur, the elixir of life and eternal youth, and expires

Page 167 – Are You Qualified?

1. The Second Doctor
2. Jo Grant
3. River Song
4. Ace
5. Clifford Jones
6. Liz Shaw
7. Mr Copper
8. Rose
9. Zoe
10. The Third Doctor
11. Cosmic Science
12. Victoria

13. The Eleventh Doctor
14. Professor Marius
15. Vicki

Page 169 – Leave Me, Doctor! Save Yourself!

1. Kath McDonnell
2. Hostess
3. Pete Tyler
4. Donna
5. Katarina
6. Guido
7. Edward Waterfield
8. Lester
9. Father Octavian
10. Luke Rattigan
11. Robert (aka John) Ashe
12. Rogin
13. Lieutenant Galloway
14. Fewsham
15. Antodus

Page 171 – Planetary Puzzles 1 – Skaro

1. 'The Dead Planet'
2. The Hand of Omega
3. Earth
4. The Master
5. The Dalek City

6. Varga plant
7. *The Evil of the Daleks*
8. 500 years
9. A forest fire
10. The Wastelands
11. Magneton
12. Darla von Karlsen
13. Twelfth
14. D5-Gamma-Z-Alpha
15. Elyon

Page 173 – Planetary Puzzles 2 – New Earth

1. The Sisters of Plenitude
2. Macra
3. Apple grass
4. The Face of Boe
5. Sally Calypso
6. Ten million
7. Thirty
8. Pharmacytown
9. Bliss
10. Seven minutes
11. Battery Park
12. Brooklyn
13. Earth on a Wednesday afternoon
14. One hundred years
15. Fifteen

Page 175 – Planetary Puzzles 3 – The Solar System

1. Mavic Chen
2. Voga (aka Neo Phobos)
3. Megropolis One
4. Titan
5. Venus
6. The Eternals
7. Uranus
8. The Flood
9. Mars
10. Two minutes
11. Jupiter
12. Gusev
13. Cassius
14. Desperus
15. Forty billion

Page 177 – Planetary Puzzles 4 – Peladon

1. Earth
2. Alpha Centauri
3. Hepesh
4. Ortron
5. Aggedor's head
6. Men of rank and females of royal blood
7. Princess Josephine of TARDIS
8. Grun
9. Arcturus
10. In the tunnels beneath the citadel

11. The Time Lords
12. Trisilicate
13. Fifty years
14. Gebek
15. Mount Megeshra

Page 179 – We've Got Your Number 1
1. 9
2. 3
3. 1
4. 40
5. 7
6. 15
7. 7
8. 7
9. 7
10. 3
11. 6
12. 14
13. 715
14. 50
15. 80

Page 181 – We've Got Your Number 2
1. 3
2. 4
3. 4

4. 76
5. 5
6. 1
7. 6
8. 123
9. 419
10. 62
11. 1489
12. 133
13. 41
14. 685
15. 982

Page 183 – Acronyms

1. Time And Relative Dimensions In Space
2. United Nations Intelligence Taskforce
3. UNified Intelligence Taskforce
4. London Investigative 'N' Detective Agency
5. Celestial Intervention Agency
6. Time And Relative Dimension In Space
7. Charlotte Abigail Lux
8. Interplanetary Mining Corporation
9. Scientific Reform Society
10. You Are Not Alone
11. Tethered Aerial Release Developed In Style
12. Transmission Of Matter Through Interstitial Time
13. Run You Clever Boy And Remember
14. Biomorphic Organisational Systems Superviser

15. Friends Of The Ood

Page 185 – I Think I'd Rather Have a Pint

1. The Cloven Hoof
2. The Rose and Crown
3. Dolly Bailey
4. The Last Chance Saloon
5. Gore Crow
6. Ian
7. Le Chien Gris
8. The Fleur de Lys
9. Jacob Kewper
10. The Sinking Ship
11. The Sea Eagle
12. Drayton Court
13. The Fox Inn
14. The Lamb and Flag
15. The Crown and Anchor

Closing Credits (2)

Page 189 – Initially – J

1. Jenny
2. Judoon
3. Jondar
4. Jethrik
5. Jago
6. Jabe
7. Jamie
8. Jellicoe
9. Jackson
10. Jobel
11. Jast
12. Jaconda
13. Jatt
14. Jano
15. Jackij

Page 190 – Initially – K

1. Kaleds
2. Key
3. Krafayis
4. Krotons

5. Kroagnon
6. Koh-i-Noor
7. Kenny
8. Kastria
9. Karkus
10. Kassia
11. Kroll
12. Kasterborous
13. Kurkutji
14. Kembel
15. Krontep

Page 191 – Initially – L

1. Lazarus
2. Leadworth
3. Logopolis
4. Lavinia
5. Llanfairfach
6. Laszlo
7. Lumic
8. Latimer
9. Logicians
10. Lungs
11. Luna
12. Laurenzi
13. Lucifer
14. Leeds
15. Lynley

Opening Titles (3)

Page 195 – Initially – M

1. Medusa
2. Mott
3. The Matrix
4. The Myrka
5. Mace
6. Mistletoe
7. Mentalis
8. Metaltron
9. Mels
10. Magpie
11. Monopticon
12. McFly
13. Morocco
14. McMillan
15. Malmooth

Page 197 – Initially – N

1. Nixon
2. Nyssa
3. Naismith
4. Nimon

5. Nyder
6. Nerva
7. Nimrod
8. Nightingale
9. Nancy
10. Noddy
11. Nucleus
12. Napoleon
13. Nuton
14. Nottingham
15. Nitrofine

Page 199 – Initially – O

1. Omega
2. Obama
3. Ood-Sphere
4. Oswin
5. Ogrons
6. Oseidon
7. Organon
8. Ostrich
9. Osiran (sometimes spelled Osirian)
10. Oracle
11. Overlords
12. Ogri
13. Om-Com
14. Oshodi
15. Orb

Episode Three
Behind the Scenes

Page 203 – The Producers
1. Russell T Davies
2. Steven Moffat
3. John Nathan-Turner
4. Verity Lambert
5. Philip Hinchcliffe
6. Graham Williams
7. Barry Letts
8. John Wiles
9. Phil Collinson
10. Innes Lloyd
11. Susie Liggat
12. Tracie Simpson
13. Derrick Sherwin
14. Marcus Wilson
15. Peter V. Ware

Page 204 – The Directors 1
1. Douglas Camfield
2. Euros Lyn
3. Michael E. Briant

4. Waris Hussein
5. Joe Ahearne
6. Dan Zeff
7. Tristan de Vere Cole
8. Toby Haynes
9. Lovett Bickford
10. Paul Joyce
11. Nick Hurran
12. Farren Blackburn
13. Michael Imison
14. Michael Owen Morris
15. Brian Grant

Page 205 – The Directors 2

1. Graeme Harper
2. Alice Troughton
3. Chris Clough
4. Hettie MacDonald
5. Keith Boak
6. Geoffrey Sax
7. John Gorrie
8. George Spenton-Foster
9. Hugh David
10. Paul Bernard
11. Darrol Blake
12. Stephen Woolfenden
13. Gerry Mill
14. Henric Hirsch

15. Michael Leeston-Smith

Page 206 – The Script Editors

1. Terrance Dicks
2. Robert Holmes
3. Douglas Adams
4. Christopher H. Bidmead
5. Eric Saward
6. David Whitaker
7. Donald Tosh
8. Andrew Cartmel
9. Helen Raynor
10. Gary Russell
11. Victor Pemberton
12. Gerry Davis
13. Elwen Rowlands
14. Lindsey Alford
15. Nikki Smith

Page 207 – The Composers

1. Tristram Cary
2. Richard Rodney Bennett
3. Malcolm Clarke
4. Murray Gold
5. Mark Ayres
6. Dominic Glynn
7. Roger Limb

8. Peter Howell
9. Geoffrey Burgon
10. Carey Blyton
11. Norman Kay
12. Richard Hartley
13. Liz Parker
14. Don Harper
15. Humphrey Searle

Page 208 – The Writers

1. Terry Nation
2. Paul Cornell
3. Brian Hayles
4. Malcolm Hulke
5. Gareth Roberts
6. Kit Pedler
7. Ben Aaronovitch
8. Ian Stuart Black
9. Robert Banks Stewart
10. Toby Whithouse
11. Neil Cross
12. Malcolm Kohll
13. William Emms
14. Peter R. Newman
15. Barbara Clegg

Page 209 – One-Hit Wonders

1. *Vincent and the Doctor*
2. *Survival*
3. *The Fires of Pompeii*
4. *Dalek*
5. *An Unearthly Child*
6. *The Mind Robber*
7. *Fury from the Deep*
8. *Ghost Light*
9. *Timelash*
10. *Amy's Choice*
11. *Planet of the Ood*
12. *Doctor Who* (TV movie)
13. *Silver Nemesis*
14. *The Underwater Menace*
15. *The Twin Dilemma*

Page 210 – Bubbling Lumps of Hate

1. John Scott Martin
2. Barnaby Edwards
3. Nicholas Pegg
4. Cy Town
5. Kevin Manser
6. Gerald Taylor
7. David Hankinson
8. Anthony Spargo
9. Tony Starr
10. Keith Ashley

11. Dan Barratt
12. Ken Tyllsen
13. Toby Byrne
14. Michael Summerton
15. Stuart Crossman

Page 211 – Working Titles 1

1. *The Web Planet*
2. *Amy's Choice*
3. *The Power of Three*
4. *Survival*
5. *The Time Meddler*
6. *Forest of the Dead*
7. *The Impossible Astronaut*
8. *Father's Day*
9. *The Shakespeare Code*
10. *Time and the Rani*
11. *Horror of Fang Rock*
12. *The Visitation*
13. *The Power of Kroll*
14. *Inferno*
15. *Night Terrors*

Page 212 – Working Titles 2

1. *The Face of Evil*
2. *The Leisure Hive*
3. *Doomsday*

4. *A Good Man Goes to War*
5. *The Tomb of the Cybermen*
6. *Genesis of the Daleks*
7. *Nightmare in Silver*
8. *Rise of the Cybermen / The Age of Steel*
9. *World War Three*
10. *The Angels Take Manhattan*
11. *Meglos*
12. *Hide*
13. *Dalek*
14. *The Masque of Mandragora*
15. *Carnival of Monsters*

Page 213 – Working Titles 3

1. 'Return to Varga'   *The Daleks' Master Plan 10*
2. 'Is There a Doctor in the Horse?'   *The Myth Makers 3*
3. 'Land of the Pharaohs'   *The Daleks' Master Plan 9*
4. 'The Four Dimensions of Time'   *The Space Museum 1*
5. 'Centre of Terror'   *The Web Planet 6*
6. 'The Caves of Terror'   *The Daleks 6*
7. 'The Paradox'   *The Time Meddler 1*
8. 'Damsel in Distress'   *The Crusade 2*
9. 'The Dawn of Knowledge'   *An Unearthly Child 4*
10. 'The Mutation of Time'   *The Daleks' Master Plan 12*
11. 'Death in the Afternoon'   *Planet of Giants 2*
12. 'Zone Seven'   *The Space Museum 4*

13. 'The Execution'   *The Daleks 7*
14. 'Changing Fortunes'   *The Crusade 3*
15. 'There's Something Just Behind You' *The Daleks' Master Plan 5*

Page 215 – By Any Other Name

1. Barbara
2. Ian
3. Steven
4. Susan
5. Vicki
6. Steven
7. Ace
8. Vicki
9. Susan
10. Vicki
11. Ben
12. Vicki
13. Jamie
14. Tegan Jovanka
15. Susan

Page 217 – Haven't I Seen You Somewhere Before? 1

1. Colin Baker
2. Peter Capaldi
3. Karen Gillan
4. Jacqueline Hill
5. Freema Agyeman

6. John Levene
7. Peter Purves
8. Ian Marter
9. Stephen Thorne
10. Ian Collier
11. Jimmy Vee
12. Edwin Richfield
13. Fiona Walker
14. David Savile
15. Peter Jeffrey

Page 218 – Haven't I Seen You Somewhere Before? 2

1. Anne Reid
2. Gabriel Woolf
3. David Troughton
4. Pauline Collins
5. Lynda Baron
6. Geoffrey Palmer
7. Margaret John
8. Christopher Benjamin
9. Clive Swift
10. Garrick Hagon
11. Colin Spaull
12. Trevor Laird
13. Jessica Martin
14. Sheila Reid
15. Bella Emberg

Page 219 – Odd One Out 1

1. *The Dominators*
2. *Carnival of Monsters*
3. *The Ice Warriors*
4. *Tooth and Claw*
5. *Planet of Giants*
6. *The Wheel in Space*
7. *Terminus*
8. *Revenge of the Cybermen*
9. *The Ark in Space*
10. *Nightmare of Eden*
11. *The Smugglers*
12. *The Web of Fear*
13. *The Masque of Mandragora*
14. *The Gunfighters*
15. *The Macra Terror*

Page 221 – Odd One Out 2

1. *Colony in Space*
2. *The Tomb of the Cybermen*
3. *The Twin Dilemma*
4. *Genesis of the Daleks*
5. *The Stones of Blood*
6. *Arc of Infinity*
7. *Planet of Evil*
8. *Terror of the Zygons*
9. *The Face of Evil*
10. *Underworld*

11. *The Invasion*
12. *Robot*
13. *Turn Left*
14. *Logopolis*
15. *The Deadly Assassin*

Page 223 – Name Share
1. John
2. Russell
3. Arthur
4. Alexander
5. Graham
6. Murphy
7. Barry
8. Bruce
9. Miles
10. Jack
11. Douglas
12. Ray
13. Adrian
14. James
15. Anton

Page 224 – Location, Location, Location 1: Home
1. *Spearhead from Space*
2. *The Faceless Ones*
3. *Time-Flight*

4. *Terror of the Autons*
5. *The Sea Devils*
6. *The Androids of Tara*
7. *The Mind of Evil*
8. *The Dalek Invasion of Earth*
9. *Smith and Jones*
10. *Mawdryn Undead*
11. *The King's Demons*
12. *Silver Nemesis*
13. *The Time Warrior*
14. *The Doctor, the Widow and the Wardrobe*
15. *Doctor Who and the Silurians*

Page 225 – Location, Location, Location 2 – Away

1. *The Fires of Pompeii*
2. *Arc of Infinity*
3. *City of Death*
4. *Daleks in Manhatten / Evolution of the Daleks*
5. *The Angels Take Manhatten*
6. *Planet of Fire*
7. *The Two Doctors*
8. *Doctor Who* (TV movie)
9. *The Impossible Astronaut / Day of the Moon*
10. *Planet of the Dead*
11. *A Town Called Mercy*
12. *The Vampires of Venice*
13. *Vincent and the Doctor*
14. Singapore

15. *The Abominable Snowmen*

Page 227 – Surprise, Surprise

1. Androgum
2. Drashig
3. Kaled (Dalek)
4. Torchwood
5. Loyhargil
6. Adric
7. Tractator
8. Tetraps
9. Osterhagen
10. Roy Tromelly (Terry Molloy – who played Davros)
11. Leon Ny Taiy (Tony Ainley – who played the Master)
12. Neil Toynay (Tony Ainley – who played the Master)
13. James Stoker (Master's joke)
14. Panic Moon (Companion)
15. Men on Waves (Woman Seven)

Page 229 – Guards, Guards

1. *Utopia*   Robert Forknall
2. *The Hand of Fear*   Robin Hargrave
3. *The Sun Makers*   Tom Kelly
4. *The Pandorica Opens* Joe Jacobs
5. *The Five Doctors*   John Tallents
6. *Fury from the Deep* Peter Ducrow
7. *Terror of the Vervoids* Hugh Beverton

8. *The Mark of the Rani*   Richard Steele
9. *The Time Monster*   Melville Jones
10. *The Keys of Marinus*   Alan James
11. *The Power of the Daleks* Robert Luckham
12. *The Macra Terror*   John Caesar
13. *The Seeds of Doom*   Harry Fielder
14. *The Pirate Planet*   Adam Kurakin
15. *The Savages*   Tim Goodman

Page 230 – Missing Episodes

1. John Cura
2. *Mission to the Unknown*
3. John Wiles
4. Hong Kong
5. Episode Three
6. *The Macra Terror*
7. Jamie
8. Ben and Polly
9. *The Mind Robber*
10. Robert Jewell
11. *The Daleks' Master Plan*
12. Bryan Mosely
13. 1978
14. *The Wall of Lies*
15. *The Highlanders*

The Answers

Page 232 – Do You Remember the First Time?
1. *Spearhead from Space*
2. *Castrovalva*
3. *The Day of the Doctor*
4. *The Reign of Terror*
5. *Spearhead from Space*
6. *Revenge of the Cybermen*
7. *The Macra Terror*
8. *Doctor Who and the Silurians*
9. *The Mind of Evil*
10. *The Time Warrior*
11. *The Ambassadors of Death*
12. *The Dalek Invasion of Earth*
13. *Robot*
14. *Planet of the Dead*
15. The Mutants

Page 233 – The Other Side of the Camera
1. *The Lazarus Experiment*
2. *The Sontaran Experiment*
3. *Arc of Infinity*
4. *Spearhead from Space*
5. *The God Complex*
6. *The Invasion*
7. *Voyage of the Damned*
8. *The Brain of Morbius*
9. *The Moonbase*
10. *The Talons of Weng-Chiang*

11. *Silver Nemesis*
12. *The Mind of Evil*
13. *The Sea Devils*
14. *The Monster of Peladon*
15. *Doctor Who and the Silurians*

Page 234 – Costume Capers 1

1. *Victory of the Daleks*
2. *The Time of the Doctor*
3. *Warriors of the Deep*
4. *Nightmare in Silver*
5. *The Hungry Earth*
6. *Closing Time*
7. *The Two Doctors*
8. *The Ribos Operation*
9. *The Armageddon Factor*
10. *Revelation of the Daleks*
11. *The Dalek Invasion of Earth*
12. *Day of the Daleks*
13. *The Wheel in Space*
14. *The Five Doctors*
15. *Daleks in Manhattan*

Page 236 – Costume Capers 2

1. *The Big Bang*
2. *Revelation of the Daleks*
3. *The Tenth Planet*

4. *Revenge of the Cybermen*
5. *The Sea Devils*
6. *Attack of the Cybermen*
7. *The Tomb of the Cybermen*
8. *The Sontaran Stratagem*
9. *Mawdryn Undead*
10. *Enlightenment*
11. *The Sontaran Experiment*
12. *The Dalek Invasion of Earth*
13. *Planet of the Daleks*
14. *The Evil of the Daleks*
15. *The Chase*

Page 238 – Dressing for the Occasion

1. Raymond Cusick
2. Cybermen
3. James Acheson
4. Drashigs
5. Shawcraft Engineering
6. Ken Trew
7. Mike Tucker
8. Millennium FX
9. June Hudson
10. John Friedlander
11. Monoids
12. Pat Godfrey
13. Christine Rawlins
14. Giant maggots

15. Howard Burden

Page 240 – Credit Crunch

1. *Logopolis*
2. *The Sea Devils*
3. *The Web Planet*
4. *The Name of the Doctor*
5. *Invasion of the Dinosaurs*
6. *The Invasion*
7. *The Green Death*
8. The Doctor
9. *Death to the Daleks*
10. *Voyage of the Damned*
11. Katharine Schlesinger
12. *Daleks in Manhattan*
13. *The Tenth Planet*
14. *Destiny of the Daleks*
15. *The Web of Fear*

Page 242 – The Men Inside the Monsters

1. Michael Kilgariff
2. Stephen Thorne
3. Pat Gorman
4. Christopher Ryan
5. Spencer Wilding
6. Paul Kasey
7. Stuart Fell

8. Jack Pitt
9. Ruari Mears
10. Nick Evans
11. Robert Jewell
12. Ian Thompson
13. Ralph Carrigan
14. Aidan Cook
15. Tony Harwood

Page 243 – The Voice

1. K-9
2. The Face of Boe
3. Cassandra
4. The Great Intelligence
5. BOSS
6. The Great One
7. The Rill
8. WOTAN
9. The Atraxi
10. The Animus
11. Morpho
12. The Empty Child
13. The Oracle
14. Arcturus
15. Bandril Ambassador

Page 244 – Ratings War

1. The Tenth Doctor
2. The Fourth Doctor
3. *Rose*
4. *Voyage of the Damned*
5. Because there was an ITV strike on at the time of broadcast
6. *City of Death* Part 4
7. *Battlefield*
8. *The Day of the Doctor, The Three Doctors, The Five Doctors, The Two Doctors*
9. *The Runaway Bride*
10. *The Dalek Invasion of Earth* Episode 2 (titled 'The Daleks')
11. *The Empty Child*
12. *The Dalek Invasion of Earth*
13. *The Ark* Episode 1 (titled 'The Steel Sky')
14. *The Daleks* Episode 6 (titled 'The Ordeal')
15. *The Ark in Space* Part 2

Page 246 – Titles and Tunes

1. Ron Grainer
2. Delia Derbyshire
3. The TARDIS
4. Murray Gold
5. *Robot*
6. Peter Howell
7. *The Ultimate Foe*
8. The Radiophonic Workshop
9. Season 23 (1986)

10. Jon Pertwee
11. *Doctor Who* (TV movie)
12. *The Three Doctors*
13. *The Snowmen*
14. *The Ambassadors of Death*
15. John Debney

Page 248 – Gossip Column

1. Georgia Moffett as Jenny (*The Doctor's Daughter*)
2. Lalla Ward as Romana
3. Jack Watling as Professor Travers (*The Abominable Snowmen / The Web of Fear*)
4. Richard Dawkins as himself (*The Stolen Earth*)
5. Michael Gough as the Celestial Toymaker (*The Celestial Toymaker*)

6. Jean Marsh as Sara Kingdom
7. Liza Goddard as Kari (*Terminus*)
8. Kismet Delgado as Spider Voice (*Planet of the Spiders*)
9. David Troughton as King Peladon (*The Curse of Peladon*)
10. Caroline John as Liz Shaw

11. Souska John as Child (*Castrovalva*)
12. Sandy McDonald as Footman (*The Unicorn and the Wasp*)
13. Julie Brennon as Fire Escape (*Paradise Towers*)
14. Jeremy Young as Gordon Lowery (*Mission to the Unknown*)
15. Richard Willis as Varsh (*Full Circle*)

Page 250 – Soap Suds 1

1. Frazer Hines
2. Kylie Minogue
3. Mary Tamm
4. Jenna Coleman (as Jenna-Louise Coleman)
5. Louise Jameson
6. Julia Smith
7. Phil Collinson
8. *EastEnders*
9. William Russell
10. Maureen O'Brien
11. *Crossroads*
12. *Revelations*
13. Richard Franklin
14. Peter Ling
15. *Springhill*

Page 252 – Soap Suds 2

1. *Resurrection of the Daleks*
2. *Colony in Space*
3. *The Time Warrior*
4. *The Daleks*
5. *Resurrection of the Daleks | Revelation of the Daleks | Remembrance of the Daleks*
6. *Kinda*
7. *Rose*
8. *Bad Wolf*
9. *The Shakespeare Code*

10. *Last of the Time Lords*
11. *The Sensorites*
12. *The Space Pirates*
13. *Terror of the Zygons*
14. *The Aztecs*
15. *The Idiot's Lantern*

Page 253 – Stage Names and Pseudonyns

1. Peter Davison
2. William Russell
3. Lalla Ward
4. David Tennant
5. Terrance Dicks, with rewrites by Robert Holmes
6. Billie Piper
7. Arthur Darvill
8. Sylvester McCoy
9. Robert Sloman and Barry Letts
10. Mervyn Haisman and Henry Lincoln
11. Janet Fielding
12. John Levene
13. Robert Holmes, rewriting an original script by Lewis Greifer
14. Graham Williams and Anthony Read
15. Douglas Adams and Graham Williams, rewriting an original script by David Fisher

Closing Credits (3)

Page 257 – Initially – P

1. Powell
2. Pig
3. Pandorica
4. Probic
5. Peg-doll
6. *Pentallian*
7. Pyroviles
8. Poppaea
9. Proper
10. Purple
11. Pigbin
12. Peru
13. Perigosto
14. Pex
15. Pallushi

Page 258 – Initially – R

1. Rassilon
2. Rift
3. Recorder
4. Robomen

5. Rutans
6. Randomiser
7. Raffalo
8. Raxacoricofallapatorius
9. Rattigan
10. Reinette
11. Rel
12. Robot
13. Rills
14. Raaga
15. Ribos

Page 259 – Initially – S

1. Salamander
2. Spartacus
3. Solomon
4. Shadow
5. Stormageddon
6. Shrivenzale
7. Sevrin
8. Shura
9. Swampies
10. Stangmoor
11. Stonehenge
12. Space
13. Skasas
14. *Skystriker*
15. Salostopus

Opening Titles (4)

Page 263 – Initially – T

1. Torchwood
2. Toclafane
3. Tritovores
4. Trilogic
5. The *Titanic*
6. *Thunderbolt*
7. Travers
8. Tetraps
9. Tracer
10. Tenza
11. Tesh
12. Trisilicate
13. Tellurians
14. Toberman
15. Truncheon

Page 265 – Initially – U

1. Unquiet
2. Unicorn
3. UNIT
4. Utopia

5. Untempered
6. Underhenge
7. ULTIMA
8. Usurian
9. Ultravox
10. Unstoffe
11. Undefeated
12. Urquhart
13. Unbelievers
14. Uvanov
15. Undercity

Page 266 – Initially – V

1. Vanessa
2. Vesuvius
3. Verney
4. Vorg
5. Vastra
6. The *Valiant*
7. Vraxoin
8. Voga
9. Validium
10. Vulcan
11. Vena
12. Vardans
13. Varl
14. Vasor
15. Vandals

Episode Four
Monsters, Villains and Aliens

Page 269 – Assault with a Deadly Weapon

1. The Nestene Consciousness
2. Slitheen
3. The Kandyman
4. Omega
5. Cybermen
6. Pyroviles
7. Robot K1
8. Cybermen
9. Silurians and Sea Devils
10. Sontarans
11. Cybermen
12. Krotons
13. Sontarans
14. The Animus
15. Vervoids

Page 270 – Name That Villain

1. Hartigan
2. Solon
3. Vaughn

4. Maxtible
5. Chase
6. Gillyflower
7. Winters
8. Van Statten
9. Stael
10. Stevens
11. Simeon
12. Dastari
13. Pike
14. Scarlioni
15. Caven

Page 271 – Who Are You?

1. Silurians
2. Ice Warriors
3. Kaleds
4. Carrionites
5. Vinvocci
6. Cryons
7. Catkind
8. Solonians
9. Argolins
10. Thals
11. Morestrans
12. Tritovores
13. Trogs
14. Aridians

15. Dulcians

Page 272 – Daleks – The 1960s 1

1. Dals
2. Bedfordshire
3. The Slyther
4. Mud from Susan's shoes
5. Anti-radiation drugs
6. Dortmun
7. Dodgems
8. Destroy all living matter
9. A million years
10. Meteorites (a cosmic storm) and plague (germ bombs)
11. Ian
12. Temmosus
13. They can move much more quickly
14. Twenty-three days
15. Vibrascopes

Page 274 – Daleks – The 1960s 2

1. Mechons
2. The Dalek Supreme
3. Flame-thrower arms
4. Vicki
5. Trantis
6. Ancient New York
7. The Intergalactic Conference of Andromeda

8. Zephon
9. The White Terror of Barbary
10. The Monk
11. A magnetised beam
12. Mice
13. Over seventy
14. The Neutronic Randomiser
15. 1,000 years

Page 276 – Daleks – The 1960s 3

1. 'I am your servant' / 'We are your servants'
2. 'Flying pests'
3. He must rescue Victoria Waterfield
4. Transmutation of metal into gold
5. Trains
6. Three
7. Static electricity
8. A Dalek's eyestalk moves
9. Feed her by force
10. Maxtible
11. 200 years
12. Resno
13. 'Why do human beings kill human beings?'
14. 144
15. Courage, pity, chivalry, friendship and compassion

Page 278 – Daleks – The 1970s 1

1. Ogrons
2. Sir Reginald Styles
3. Dalekanium
4. To reveal an invisible Dalek
5. The Time Lords
6. The Supreme Council
7. A mind-analysis machine
8. It might trigger an automatic distress call
9. No more than twelve
10. 10,000
11. Light-ray emissions on living tissue
12. High-frequency radio impulses
13. A bacterial culture that will destroy all living tissue
14. *The Power of the Daleks*
15. The Time Vortex Magnetron

Page 280 – Daleks – The 1970s 2

1. Mark III Travel Machines
2. A relief ship from Earth
3. His hat
4. So he could break them out of the stalemate in their war against the Movellans
5. When power is restored
6. A model TARDIS
7. Two years
8. His father was killed in the last Dalek war
9. A prison ship in space

10. More than half a megaton
11. Ronson
12. Millions on Dalek colony worlds are dying from the disease that parrinium can cure
13. To force the space powers to accede to their demands
14. It discovers its prisoner (Jill Tarrant) has escaped
15. Fire a plague missile on to the planet's surface

Page 282 – Daleks – The 1980s

1. Bonded polycarbite armour
2. Commander Lytton
3. The eyepiece
4. He puts it in the casket of the Hand of Omega
5. Special Weapons Dalek
6. An ultrasonic beam of rock and roll
7. Imperial
8. Small
9. Two
10. Stein
11. They have placed duplicates in strategic positions around the planet
12. They are to be reconditioned to obey the will of the Supreme Dalek
13. Nitro-9
14. They develop a virus that exclusively attacks Daleks
15. Dalek hunting

Page 284 – Daleks – 2005 onwards 1

1. Rose's
2. Dalek Sec
3. They are turned into Pig-Slaves
4. Emergency Temporal Shift
5. Mickey Smith
6. One second
7. Simmons
8. A time lock
9. The Cage
10. To imagine new ways of Dalek survival
11. Dalek Thay
12. Gamma
13. Dalek Caan
14. The Cruciform
15. Captain Jack

Page 286 – Daleks – 2005 onwards 2

1. The Emperor Dalek
2. Dalek Caan
3. Auton Rory
4. Yellow
5. A spanner
6. Pure Dalek DNA
7. It saw them as impure
8. They had survived encounters with the Doctor
9. Carries out a mass delete, making them forget the Doctor
10. A chronon loop

11. Z-Neutrino energy
12. Bastic bullets
13. A Z-Neutrino biological inversion catalyser
14. Angie and Artie Maitland
15. 'The Emperor Dalek's New Clothes'

Page 288 – Davros 1

1. Executioner
2. Tasembeker
3. His hand
4. The Great Healer
5. The Daleks' universal supremacy
6. Kiston
7. Orcini
8. He is to be taken back to Skaro to stand trial for crimes against the Daleks
9. The head of a new Dalek army
10. Vogel's bones
11. Deep in the catacombs
12. Mutant humanoid
13. He is to be put in a cryogenic freezer and taken to stand trial for crimes against the whole of sentient creation
14. Napoleon
15. Ninety years

Page 290 – Davros 2

1. Dalek Caan

2. A cell of Davros's body
3. The Reality Bomb
4. Sarah Jane Smith
5. Gharman
6. Skaro's sun
7. The Nightmare Child
8. Dalek Caan
9. Less than thirty seconds
10. They are turned into concentrated protein food
11. The Gates of Elysium
12. The Tenth Doctor and Rose
13. Ordinary people
14. Destroyer of Worlds
15. The results of Davros's mutation experiments on animals

Page 292 – Prehistoric monsters!

1. The Brontosaurus
2. The Silurians
3. Adric
4. Tricey
5. A plesiosaurus
6. Tyrannosaurus Rex
7. A Tyrannosaurus Rex
8. A golf ball
9. Pterodactyls
10. Donna
11. A dinosaur tooth to take home
12. Lift music

13. (a) Spinosaurus
14. The Rani
15. Pink

Page 294 – Mythical Monsters 1 – Vampires

1. The Three Who Rule
2. Venice
3. A Plasmavore
4. Haemovores
5. Adric
6. Into E-Space
7. To provide brides for her sons
8. Seventeen
9. The use of bow ships
10. The Saturnynes
11. Souls
12. *The Claws of Axos*
13. The Festival of Ghana
14. Ogri
15. A UV light

Page 296 – Mythical Monsters 2 – Werewolves

1. Captain Cook
2. Professor Sorenson
3. Harry Slocum
4. Mistletoe garlands
5. Light rays from the Moon

6. Haemophilia
7. Prince Albert
8. Vulpana
9. A moon-shaped light
10. The werewolf biting Queen Victoria
11. Dorf (the Lukoser)
12. 1540
13. The Destroyer
14. A lupine wavelength haemovariform
15. *Viscum album* (mistletoe oil)

Page 298 – Mythical Monsters 3 – Minotaur
1. 'Praise him'
2. The Power Complex
3. Ian
4. Fear
5. 'The Minotaur is a mythical beast. It doesn't exist.'
6. The Kronos crystal
7. Its horns
8. Amy's faith in him
9. The Great Journey of Life
10. Hippias
11. A ball of string
12. Hymetusite
13. He wanted the strength of the bull and a long life in which to use it
14. *The Wedding of River Song*
15. Pasiphae

Page 300 – Monsters and Aliens – The 1960s

1. Polly
2. His world is destroyed
3. The Menoptra
4. Hearing
5. Maaga
6. Mental power
7. Ammonia
8. Mira
9. Quarks
10. Professor Brett
11. Mire Beasts
12. Julius Silverstein
13. A gigantic explosion on their planet
14. Screamers
15. A sonic laser sound wave (made from Victoria's screams)

Page 301 – Monsters and Aliens – The 1970s

1. Daemons
2. Alpha Centauri
3. Twelve
4. Vardans
5. Axonite
6. Vega
7. Arnold Keeler
8. Tyrum and Vorus
9. Poisonus fungi
10. The end of the twentieth century

11. Horda
12. A thousand million years
13. The servo-junction unit
14. One of Grundle's satellites
15. Clark

Page 303 – Monsters and Aliens – The 1980s

1. Gavrok
2. Kitlings
3. Urbankan
4. Mestor
5. Grig
6. Sil
7. Marriner
8. Oxygen
9. The bio-mechanoid
10. Gilbert M
11. Plasmatons
12. Ultraviolet rays
13. Necros
14. A xerophyte
15. The Malus

Page 304 – Monsters and Aliens – 2005–2009

1. Victor Kennedy
2. Adipose
3. The Toclafane

4. Hath
5. Its hind brain
6. The Wire
7. Three months
8. Lonely Assassins
9. He is a cyborg
10. Christopher
11. Max
12. Their liana
13. Venom grubs
14. A-positive
15. Really long necks

Page 306 – Monsters and Aliens – 2010 onwards

1. Ood
2. Flesh
3. Silurians
4. The Whisper Men
5. A Cyberman
6. Winders
7. Kahler-Jex
8. Spoonheads
9. The (repulsive) red leech
10. Lower his hood
11. 'You should kill us all on sight.'
12. The Shakri
13. Cybermites
14. The Sunsingers of Akhat

15. The Church at Auvers

Page 307 – A Policy of Non-Intervention
1. Exile to Earth
2. The Elixir of Life
3. Solos
4. The Time Scoop
5. The Hand of Omega (a remote stellar manipulator)
6. Miniscope
7. The Andromeda Sleepers
8. Crozier
9. The De-mat gun
10. He is dematerialised
11. The Genesis Ark
12. The Minyans
13. A Metamorphic Symbiosis Regenerator
14. Validium
15. A Magnetron

Page 309 – Cybermen – The 1960s 1
1. Emotions
2. They disintegrate
3. His head is hurt so he cannot be converted
4. Fifty pounds
5. In the sickbay beds
6. The Cybermen cutting an entry hole in the storeroom
7. Professor Parry

8. Use it to change the weather to destroy the surface of the Earth
9. The Cybermen do not feel pain
10. Five centuries
11. Fred
12. The Z-Bomb
13. Radioactivity
14. Ralph (number 14)
15. Neurotrope X (a large neurotropic virus)

Page 311 – Cybermen – The 1960s 2

1. St Paul's Cathedral
2. Fear
3. Planet 14
4. The Cyberman Controller
5. Eric Klieg
6. Human brain waves
7. Billy Bug
8. The Cybermen are going to poison the air supply
9. Quick-set plastic
10. The Cerebratron Mentor
11. Private Perkins
12. Five years
13. Alpha meson phosphor
14. Bernalium
15. High-current phase contrast

Page 313 – Cybermen – The 1970s and 1980s

1. A black head with silver face
2. Gold coins and a catapult
3. Cyber Lieutenant
4. Kellman
5. Gold-tipped arrows
6. Halley's Comet
7. It is injected by a Cybermat's 'bite'
8. The dark side of the Moon
9. Stratton
10. The Cyber Controller
11. Karl
12. Richard Maynarde
13. Ringway
14. Planets are to sign a pact uniting their military forces in a war against the Cyber race
15. *The Tomb of the Cybermen* and *Revenge of the Cybermen*

Page 315 – Cybermen – 2005 onwards

1. In Henry Van Statten's collection in the Vault
2. John Lumic
3. Jackie Tyler's birthday party
4. The Cyber-converted Yvonne Hartman
5. Miss Hartigan
6. Sally Phelan
7. Crane
8. The Void ship
9. Three million

10. It is downloaded into another Cyberman
11. 15 Latimer Street
12. An arm
13. The Cyberiad
14. Mr Clever
15. 'Inelegant'

Page 317 – The Master – The 1970s 1
1. Goodge
2. Jo
3. The Doctor laughing at him
4. A horsebox
5. The Adjudicator
6. 'Mary Had a Little Lamb'
7. Rex Farrel
8. Captain Chin Lee
9. Axos
10. Episode 4
11. Switzerland
12. His TARDIS's dematerialisation circuit
13. Bill Filer
14. One must rule or serve
15. Canon Smallwood

Page 319 – The Master – The 1970s 2
1. Ruth Ingram and Stuart Hyde
2. Ogrons

3. A shrunken technician in the public register news camera
4. Hypnotism
5. Queen Galleia
6. A colour television set
7. From stolen Time Lord files
8. *The War of the Worlds*
9. Sleep gas is released
10. Hitler and Genghis Khan
11. Mathematics
12. Tersurus
13. Dr Percival
14. Sirius IV
15. Pull the wings off a fly

Page 321 – The Master – The 1980s

1. Melkur
2. Adric
3. Kamelion
4. An iron maiden
5. The Third Doctor
6. The Portreeve
7. A fireplace
8. The Concorde passengers
9. A full and free pardon, and a complete new life cycle
10. The Cybermen
11. The Seal of the High Council
12. Zarak
13. The Comparator

14. Light Speed Overdrive
15. None of them. (Kamelion-Master uses it once in *Planet of Fire*, but the Master never says it at all.)

Page 323 – The Master – The 1980s and 1990s

1. 'Bad cat man'
2. 'Won't you show mercy to your own—'
3. Bruce the ambulance driver
4. Yellow
5. Mel and Glitz
6. The Rani's TARDIS
7. Numismaton gas
8. Miasimia Goria
9. Luke Ward
10. The Key of Rassilon
11. Genghis Khan
12. A statue of Queen Victoria
13. So she can extract Peri's brain fluid
14. A fire extinguisher
15. Limbo atrophier

Page 325 – The Master – 2005 onwards

1. Lucy Saxon
2. The Immortality Gate
3. Chantho
4. Martha
5. Donna

6. Because he would be the perfect warrior for a Time War
7. Martha
8. To create a link between the Master and time-locked Gallifrey
9. Miss Trefusis
10. A paradox machine
11. On the coast of the Silver Devastation
12. The Cabinet
13. Rugby Blue
14. President-Elect Winters
15. *Love & Monsters*

Page 327 – Anagrams 1

1. Myrka
2. Ergon
3. Aggedor
4. Isolus
5. Cybershade
6. Magma Beast
7. Great Vampire
8. Krafayis
9. Destroyer
10. Star Whale
11. Sentreal
12. Black Guardian
13. Great Intelligence
14. Nestene Consciousness
15. Alpha Centauri

Page 328 – Anagrams 2

1. Sea Devil
2. Sontaran
3. Sycorax
4. Krillitane
5. Plasmavore
6. Cybermat
7. Mandrel
8. Carrionite
9. Tractator
10. Vashta Nerada
11. Varga Plant
12. Skarasen
13. Menoptra
14. Mire Beast
15. Futurekind

Page 329 – Anagrams 3

1. Monoid
2. Silence
3. Trog
4. Kraal
5. Pyrovile
6. Saturnyne
7. Gastropod
8. Haemovore
9. Chameleon
10. Adipose

11. Toclafane
12. Mandragora Helix
13. Plasmaton
14. Fendahl
15. Weeping Angel

Page 330 – Anagrams 4

1. Cryon
2. Thal
3. Sensorite
4. Draconian
5. Solonian
6. Silurian
7. Ice Warrior
8. Bandril
9. Aridian
10. Eternal
11. Tritovore
12. Morestran
13. Usurian
14. Tythonian
15. Refusian

Closing Credits (4)

Page 333 – Initially – W
1. The Wire
2. Wirrn
3. White
4. Weeping
5. Webstar
6. Wells
7. Wenley
8. Worm
9. The Watcher
10. Whizzkid
11. Warlock
12. Widow
13. Wallscrawlers
14. Wilson
15. Wester

Page 335 – Initially – QXY
1. Quarks
2. Yartek
3. Yeti
4. Xoanon

5. Question
6. Quinn
7. Xanxia
8. Xeros
9. Yana
10. The Quest
11. Xeraphin
12. Yo-yo
13. Quiquaequod
14. Quinnis
15. Xana

Page 337 – Initially – Z

1. Zarbi
2. Zeus
3. Zygons
4. Zoe
5. Zaroff
6. Zu-zanna
7. Zadek
8. Zanak
9. Zocci
10. Zed
11. Zaffic
12. Zigma
13. Zilda
14. Zondal
15. Zucker

Next-Time Trailer

Page 341 – Missing Vowels 1 – Story Titles

1. *The Ark*
2. *Frontios*
3. *Closing Time*
4. *The Invasion*
5. *Fear Her*
6. *The Ice Warriors*
7. *Planet of Evil*
8. *Amy's Choice*
9. *Evolution of the Daleks*
10. *The Seeds of Death*
11. *The Ultimate Foe*
12. *Utopia*
13. *Time and the Rani*
14. *Planet of the Ood*
15. *The Fires of Pompeii*

Page 342 – Missing Vowels 2 – Episode Titles

1. 'The Edge of Destruction'
2. 'The Velvet Web'
3. 'Inferno
4. 'Airlock'

5. 'An Unearthly Child'
6. 'The Death of Doctor Who
7. 'Crisis'
8. 'Escape to Danger'
9. 'The Celestial Toyroom'
10. 'The Waking Ally'
11. 'The OK Corral'
12. 'A Change of Identity'
13. 'The Ordeal'
14. 'The Unwilling Warriors'
15. 'Assassin at Peking'

Page 343 – Gold Run

1. New New York
2. Space Security Service
3. Headless Monks
4. Jack the Ripper
5. Vashta Nerada
6. Forest of Cheem
7. Cup of Athelstan
8. Chessene o' the Franzine Grig
9. Fob watch
10. Tower of London
11. Security Kitchen
12. Mighty Jagrafess of the Holy Hadrojassic Maxarodenfoe
13. Mrs Golightly's Happy Travelling University and Dry Cleaners
14. *Bear with Me*

15. *Bartholomew's Planetary Gazetteer*

Page 345 – Adding a Bit 1

1. Time
2. Sea
3. Black
4. Queen
5. Sonic
6. Silver
7. War
8. Great
9. Psychic
10. Cyber
11. Liz (or LIZ)
12. Captain
13. Chief
14. Fire
15. Mind

Page 346 – Adding a Bit 2

1. Factor
2. War
3. Experiment
4. Moor
5. Minor
6. Planet
7. Robot

8. People
9. Chase
10. School
11. Sky
12. End
13. Bomb
14. Base
15. Warrior

Page 347 – Adding a Bit 3

1. Wolf
2. Storm
3. Game
4. Time
5. Fear
6. Death
7. Marshall
8. Demons
9. Gun
10. Leader
11. Alpha
12. Mother
13. King
14. Ring
15. Fire

Page 348 – Quote Unquote

1. *The Seeds of Doom | The End of Time*
2. *The Five Doctors | The Three Doctors*
3. *Dragonfire | Battlefield*
4. *The Dalek Invasion of Earth | The Wheel in Space*
5. *City of Death | Dinosaurs on a Spaceship*
6. *Revenge of the Cybermen | Evolution of the Daleks*
7. *A Christmas Carol | The Runaway Bride*
8. *Genesis of the Daleks | The Pirate Planet*
9. *The Invisible Enemy | Human Nature*
10. *The Five Doctors | The Moonbase*
11. *The Mutants | The Hand of Fear*
12. *The Talons of Weng-Chiang | The Lodger*
13. *The Enemy of the World | Full Circle*
14. *Survival | Inferno*
15. *Image of the Fendahl | The Underwater Menace*

Page 351 – Two's Company

1. *The Fires of Pompeii*
2. *The Krotons* and *Cold War*
3. The Third and the Ninth Doctors
4. *The Enemy of the World* and *The Web of Fear* (Patrick and David Troughton; Deborah and Jack Watling)
5. *The Mind of Evil* and *Carnival of Monsters*
6. Hale and Pace (*Survival*) and Mitchell and Webb (*Dinosaurs on a Spaceship*)
7. 'An Unearthly Child' and 'The Dead Planet' (Episode 1 of *The Daleks*)

8. *The Space Museum* and *Invasion of the Dinosaurs*
9. *Galaxy 4* and *42*
10. Solon and Shockeye
11. The Third and the Ninth Doctors
12. *The Underwater Menace* and *The Moonbase*
13. Harry and K-9 Mk II
14. *Mawdryn Undead* and *The Five Doctors*
15. Eleanor Bron

Page 353 – Connect 3

1. All hide inside a Dalek casing
2. The names the Second Doctor gives to the humanised Daleks
3. The Earth is destroyed
4. Saxon (The Master's diaries, played by James, a Saxon in *The Time Meddler*)
5. Jo's visions from the fear device in *Frontier in Space*
6. Names used to differentiate *The Chase*'s Fungoids in rehearsals (Fungoid Fred, Toadstool Taffy, Mushroom Malone)
7. Clips from them are featured in *The War Games*
8. Played Romana's discarded bodies in *Destiny of the Daleks*
9. Recited by Jo to stop the Master hypnotising her in *Frontier in Space*
10. All are controlled with a bracelet
11. The exact same character is played by two different, credited actors over the course of a story
12. Places where bugs are hidden (*Terror of the Zygons*, *The Android*

Invasion, The Power of the Daleks)

13. Ships / spaceships that the Doctor has been on
14. Their fathers are killed in their first stories
15. All given pet names by Vicki

Page 354 – Connect 4

1. All feature unreal worlds
2. Gold (planet of, surname, title, surname)
3. All were blank-faced
4. Noted as the last of their races (Jagaroth, Zolfa-Thuran, Time Lord, Boekind)
5. Aliases of Cessair of Diplos
6. All mute characters
7. All mention or feature Metebelis 3
8. Master (Le Maitre, 'worthy of the Master', Master Brain, *The Dalek's Master Plan*)
9. Human companions who are never given a surname onscreen
10. Each is seen driving an ambulance
11. Mutant (episode title, also known as, roles credited as)
12. All visited by the Rani
13. All are seen to eat bananas
14. Slade's 'Merry Xmas Everybody' can be heard in all of them
15. Shapes of Voord antennae

Page 356 – Connect 5

1. A single eye

2. All guises adopted by the Master
3. Colours of the Paradigm Daleks
4. All live on planets whose names we never discover
5. Add 'yard' to find names the Doctor called the Valeyard
6. Clowns (in *The Celestial Toymaker*, called by First Doctor, builds robot ones, sad one found inside in *The God Complex*, credited as)
7. All come in Venusian versions
8. All named in credits but not within the story itself
9. All are zones in *The War Games*
10. *Blue Peter* (design competition winner, presenter roles, featured in episode, role won in competition)
11. Planet samples stored on the CET machine (*Nightmare of Eden*)
12. Commonly used names that are never given on screen (including in credits)
13. Injured ankles
14. All were broadcast with a different number of episodes to originally planned
15. Companions whose first appearance wasn't in Episode 1 of their debut story

Page 358 – What Comes Next?

1. A Taran statue (pieces of the Key to Time in collection order)
2. The Brothers Hop Pyleen (guests on Platform One in arrival order)
3. *The Chase* (feature Daleks)
4. Paul McGann (actor's age on *Doctor Who* debut from

youngest)

5. Stetson (new hats adopted by the Eleventh Doctor)
6. Lynda Moss (the people whom Davros says have died in the Doctor's name, in flashback order)
7. *The Daleks' Master Plan* (scenes set on contemporary Earth)
8. *The Mutants* (the Third Doctor leaves Earth)
9. *Meglos* (lowest average viewing figures per Doctor)
10. Exterminated (deaths of the members of the Galactic Council)
11. *The Mysterious Planet* (debuts of new complete TARDIS police-box props)
12. *The Reign of Terror* Episodes 2 and 3 (main cast member holidays)
13. *The Power of the Daleks* (had *Radio Times* covers)
14. Metebelis 3 (planets the TARDIS lands on for a second time post-*An Unearthly Child*)
15. Sea Devils (biggest gap in years between debut and return)

Page 359 – Titles Within Titles 1
1. *The Evil of the Daleks*
2. *The Daemons*
3. *The Smugglers*
4. *Invasion of the Dinosaurs*
5. *Genesis of the Daleks*
6. *Planet of Fire*
7. *Survival*
8. *The Crusade*
9. *The Time Monster*

10. *The Web of Fear*
11. *The Mutants*
12. *The Tenth Planet*
13. *The Underwater Menace*
14. *The Wheel in Space*
15. *Carnival of Monsters*

Page 361 – Titles Within Titles 2

1. *Evolution of the Daleks*
2. *Voyage of the Damned*
3. *The Fires of Pompeii*
4. *Day of the Moon*
5. *The Runaway Bride*
6. *Journey's End*
7. *The Name of the Doctor*
8. *Vincent and the Doctor*
9. *The Waters of Mars*
10. *Asylum of the Daleks*
11. *The Wedding of River Song*
12. *The Unquiet Dead*
13. *Journey to the Centre of the TARDIS*
14. *42*
15. *Midnight*

Page 363 – Titles Within Titles 3

1. *The End of Time, Part One*
2. *The Shakespeare Code*

3. *Silence in the Library*
4. *The Name of the Doctor*
5. *The Next Doctor*
6. *The Unquiet Dead*
7. *Rose*
8. *The Sontaran Stratagem*
9. *The Snowmen*
10. *The Stolen Earth*
11. *42*
12. *Voyage of the Damned*
13. *Blink*
14. *The Wedding of River Song*
15. *The Power of Three*

Page 365 – Problematic Production Codes

1. *Robot*
2. *Fear Her*
3. *Cold Blood*
4. *Boom Town*
5. *New Earth*
6. *Marco Polo*
7. *The Myth Makers*
8. *Terror of the Autons*
9. *Horror of Fang Rock*
10. *Vengeance on Varos*
11. *The Doctor Dances*
12. *The Power of Three*
13. *Mawdryn Undead*

14. *The Angels Take Manhattan*
15. *The Tomb of the Cybermen*

Page 367 – Metamorphoses

1. ACE – GRACE
2. TEGAN – TEGANA
3. ASTRA – VASTRA
4. PERI – PERIVALE
5. AXON – SAXON
6. THAL – THALIRA
7. TARA – SONTARAN
8. SIL – SILURIAN
9. SOLON – SOLONIAN
10. BEN – BENNETT
11. IAN – VISIAN
12. RILL – KRILLITANE
13. MEL – CHAMELEON
14. RAGO – MANDRAGORA
15. TA – RUTAN

And Now on BBC One...

Page 373 – The End

1. Snakedance

Acknowledgements

Many, many thanks to the supremely trivially minded Simon Belcher, Robert Dick, Nick Farrow, James Goss, Toby Hadoke, Will Howells, Jonathan Morris, Nicholas Pegg, Ian Potter, Justin Richards, Gary Russell, Peter Ware and Mark Wright for their invaluable help.